super food ideas
Australia's top-selling food magazine

DINNER IN A DASH

Quick, easy and delicious family favourites from
Australia's bestselling food magazine

HarperCollins*Publishers*

CONTENTS

DINNER IN A DASH

No matter whether we're feeding our family, our friends, or a crowd, we all want to cook delicious food that's also quick and easy to make. At *Super Food Ideas*, Australia's top-selling food magazine, we understand this very well so every month we serve up a fresh batch of simple and clever meal ideas to inspire home cooks around the country. *Dinner in a Dash* is a collection of our fastest midweek main courses designed to make meal planning simpler and dinner something that everyone can look forward to at the end of a busy day – including the cook!

In this book you'll find our best everyday dishes, all on the table in around 45 minutes. From great ideas for soups and salads to roasts and stir-fries, you'll also find plenty of smart shortcuts and cooking tips that help you save time, energy and money. There's even a chapter dedicated to super-speedy desserts for a little midweek indulgence. In fact, there's no reason at all why you wouldn't use *Dinner in a Dash* at weekends, either. There's plenty here to enjoy on a Saturday night or Sunday lunchtime, too…

COOKING STAPLES

Make your pantry and fridge your time-saving allies.
Stock up on essential items when they're on special so you save money – and time.

ON THE SHELF

Canned vegetables – tomatoes, chickpeas, cannellini beans, kidney beans, lentils, corn kernels and baby corn, and beetroot. A can of tomatoes is the base for so many dishes – from a simple pasta sauce to a rich braise, while pulses add protein and fibre to soups, salads and vegetarian dishes. Corn kernels can be used straight from the can in salads and salsas, while beetroot can be easily turned into a relish or add colour to a salad or burger.

Canned fish – tuna and salmon are both extremely versatile and can be the basis for many a meal including quiche, pasta sauces and bakes, and fresh salads. They are also healthy, protein powerhouses. A jar of anchovies in oil can be used to top a pizza, add depth of flavour to a tomato pasta sauce or in a classic Caesar or Nicoise salad.

Stock – chicken, beef, vegetable. Chicken stock is a great base for risottos or a quick-fix soup. Just add noodles, cooked chicken and that can of corn for a simple Chinese-style soup, or add canned beans and tomatoes and other vegetables for a minestrone-style one. Use beef stock to add flavour to stir-fries or add to pan juices for a rich gravy. Vegetable stock can substitute for either.

Pasta – long, such as spaghetti and fettuccine; short, such as penne, shells or farfalle; instant lasagne sheets. Remember the simple rule – long pasta suits finer, more liquid sauces; short pasta loves a chunkier sauce. But also remember that rules are made to be broken!

Dried noodles – rice, wheat and soba – for stir-fries, wholesome Asian soups and spicy salads.

Grains – rice (basmati, jasmine, Arborio), couscous, polenta, and some of the more unusual ones, such as quinoa and bulgur (cracked wheat) – great as the base for substantial salads as well as sides.

Nuts and seeds – pine nuts, flaked almonds and walnuts for salads, pastas and sweets; sesame, pumpkin (pepita) seeds for Asian dishes and to give added crunch and goodness to salads, slices and stir-fries.

Dried fruit – cranberries, currants and sultanas, for savoury and sweet dishes. Toss dried cranberries or currants through a couscous with chopped fresh coriander, finely grated lemon rind and cumin for an instant Middle Eastern side.

Oils – apart from your everyday cooking oil, keep extra virgin olive oil and sesame oil for drizzling and dressings.

Vinegars – balsamic for salad dressings and adding warmth to tomato-based sauces; rice wine vinegar for Asian dishes and dipping sauces; white and red wine vinegar for mixing with oil for classic salad dressings.

Capers – chopped and mixed with fresh herbs and olive oil for a salsa verde (green sauce), or fried and scattered over grilled fish or chicken – they're perfect little flavour bombs.

Antipasto vegetables – artichokes, olives, semi- or sun-dried tomatoes, grilled capsicum and eggplant. Add them to pizza toppings, stir them through pasta, or jazz up salads and sandwiches. Many of these are available fresh from supermarket deli sections, too.

IN THE FRIDGE

Eggs – the ultimate go-to, super-nutritious convenience food. Whip up an omelette and fill it with chopped herbs and grated cheese, or pour lightly beaten eggs over leftover vegies in a frying pan and finish under the grill for an instant frittata. Hard-boil a few and keep to add to anything from salads and sandwiches to Malaysian-style curries.

Condiments – tapenade, mayonnaise, chilli sauce, mustard and pesto – add layers of flavour and texture.

Cured and smoked meats – bacon, prosciutto, chorizo, salami – delicious as the hero of a dish, but great flavour enhancers, too, for pasta sauces, salads and soups.

Cheese – Parmesan, fetta, cheddar, haloumi, mozzarella – must-haves for pastas, pizzas, salads and sandwiches. Fetta really adds zing to green salads, while grated Parmesan and mozzarella make for fabulous pasta bakes. Haloumi keeps for months in the fridge so is a great staple to pull out when people drop in or as a starter with fresh lemon squeezed on it.

IN THE FREEZER

Frozen peas, broad beans and corn – quick-fix vegies to add to all kinds of cooking or just to have as sides.

Pizza bases – easy, family-friendly and handy for unexpected guests.

Shortcrust and puff pastry – for free-form tarts, quick quiches and pot pies, savoury and sweet.

Vanilla ice-cream – soften it slightly and swirl through crumbled honeycomb, grated chocolate, passionfruit or whatever's handy for an instant dessert.

SHORTCUT IDEAS

With a few clever ingredients and a bit of planning ahead dinner will be ready in a dash

SIMPLE FLAVOUR BOOSTERS

Citrus – whether it's a squeeze of lemon or lime juice over fish or chicken, or grated lemon zest stirred through a risotto or sprinkled over a rich, meaty casserole, citrus lifts and enhances flavours. Orange juice and zest make a lovely base for a chicken marinade.

Herbs – parsley, coriander, basil, rosemary, oregano, thyme, bay leaves – to add fragrance and complexity. The first three, soft-leafed, herbs should be added just before serving for maximum intensity. Grow them in the backyard, on the balcony or on the windowsill – there's nothing nicer than picking them as you need them.

Aromatics – onions, garlic, ginger, fresh chillies – alone or in varying combinations, these magical ingredients form the flavour base of cuisines from every corner of the world.

Spices – start with the basics; salt (use it sparingly to lift flavours), black pepper, cumin (warm, earthy and perfect for Middle Eastern and Indian dishes), chilli flakes, ground coriander (very different from its fresh cousin), smoked paprika, Chinese five-spice and nutmeg.

FAST CUTS

Choose the right cut of meat or poultry to reduce cooking time. As a general rule, any cut of meat with bones in, such as a chicken Maryland or drumstick, will take longer to cook. To quickly roast or barbecue larger, or whole, pieces of meat, such as a leg of lamb, or whole chicken, you need to ensure the surface area in contact with the heat is maximised. Removing the bone, in the case of a leg of lamb or pork, and flattening it (butterflying), and removing the backbone and flattening out a chicken (spatchcocking or butterflying) will minimise cooking time. Marinating with ingredients such as citrus, vinegar or wine will help tenderise meat and assist in speedy cooking. The following cuts are recommended for quick results:

Chicken – mince, thigh fillet, wing, breast, drumstick, lovely leg, tenderloin, sausage.

Beef and veal – mince, stir-fry strips, steak cuts such as minute, rump, sirloin and scotch fillet, sausage, schnitzel.

Lamb – mince, backstrap/eye of loin, chump chop, loin chop, cutlet, stir-fry strips, sausage.

Pork – mince, leg steak, cutlet, butterfly steak, loin chop, fillet, stir-fry strips, forequarter chop, sausage.

COOKING TIME-SAVERS

Plan ahead. Think about what you can whip up with leftover meat and vegies then add any extra ingredients you'll need to your shopping list.

Think big. Double quantities for soups, curries, pasta sauces and bakes, then freeze them in meal-sized containers. Do the same for dressings and store them in a jar in the fridge. Make batches of pesto and freeze individual portions in ice-cube trays. Do the same with herbed butter (mash up butter with chopped fresh herbs such as parsley, thyme and rosemary) for an instant meat, chicken or fish sauce.

Salad dressing. Seal the ingredients in a jar and shake to combine then store any leftovers in the fridge for next time.

Cooking pasta. Add vegies to the water in the last couple of minutes of cooking.

Spice it up. Stock up on packaged dried spice blends and pastes to add instant zip to simple grills, roasts, steamed vegies and stir-fries.

Give chopping the chop. Tear salad leaves and herbs, or use kitchen scissors to snip chives and dill; crumble fetta or tear bocconcini straight over salads, pasta and pizza; scrub potatoes and sweet potatoes and cook with their skins on.

Microwave it. Melt butter and chocolate, steam vegies, toast breadcrumbs, nuts, seeds and whole spices, poach eggs, warm up tortillas, pita and Turkish bread, and fast-track jacket potatoes.

BE PREPARED

The French culinary phrase is *mise en place* (pronounced meez on plass), which literally means 'put in place', and it's the mantra for all organised cooks. Whether you're whipping up a Monday night spag bol or working in a Michelin-starred restaurant, it's important to get everything ready before you start. Cooking's a whole lot easier and far less stressful if you're well organised, so here's how to get the best out of any recipe, and make it easy on yourself!

Read the recipe at least once – all the way through – before you start cooking. If the recipe requires you to preheat the oven – make sure you do.

Get out any equipment you need that may be stored in a cupboard or drawer so it's to hand when you need it. There's nothing worse than fossicking through kitchen drawers with floury/buttery hands!

If possible, measure out, then chop/slice/grate/shred all your ingredients (make like the TV chefs and put them into separate containers if you can) then line them up on the bench in the order they appear in the recipe. This may seem a bit fussy, but it works!

Now you can get cooking – and we guarantee that those few minutes you've spent on *mise en place* will be well worth the effort.

CONVERSIONS

We use Australian standard measures.

In liquid measures, 250ml = 1 cup.

Dry ingredients should be measured in level 1 cup, ½ cup, ⅓ cup and ¼ cup measures.

1 tablespoon = 20ml (note NZ, US and UK tablespoon = 15ml).

1 teaspoon = 5ml.

We use 59g to 60g eggs.

We use 1000 watt microwaves, unless otherwise specified.

NUTRITION KNOW-HOW

Gluten-free: contains no wheat, oats, rye or barley.

Heart-friendly: low saturated fat, high fibre, lower sodium with heart-friendly fats.

Diabetes-friendly: low saturated fat, high fibre (not for desserts), lower sodium with lower-GI carbs.

Lower GI: contains foods with slowly digested carbohydrate(s), which produce a lower rise in your blood sugar level.

Healthy: Saturated fat must be < 6g; kilojoules < 3000kJ; sodium < 800mg. contains > 5g of fibre per main meal

	LOW FAT	LOW SAT FAT	LOWER SODIUM	LOW KILOJULE
Main meal	< 15g	< 6g	< 600mg	< 2000kJ
Side dish	< 8g	< 3g	< 400mg	<1000kJ
Light meal	< 10g	< 4g	< 400mg	< 1500kJ
Snack/dessert	< 5g	< 2g	< 200mg	< 600kJ

VEGETARIAN

SOFT POLENTA WITH MUSHROOM RAGOUT

SERVES 4
PREP 15 minutes
COOK 15 minutes

50g butter
1 leek, trimmed, halved, thinly sliced
600g mixed mushrooms, trimmed, sliced (see note)
¾ cup dry red wine
1 tablespoon finely chopped fresh rosemary
¼ cup chopped fresh flat-leaf parsley leaves
1 teaspoon caster sugar
Extra grated parmesan, to serve

Polenta

2 cups milk
2 cups vegetable stock
1 cup fine polenta
⅓ cup finely grated parmesan

1 Melt half the butter in a large frying pan over medium heat. Add leek. Cook, stirring, for 2 minutes or until starting to soften. Increase heat to high. Add mushroom. Cook, stirring, for 5 minutes or until browned. Add wine and rosemary. Bring to the boil. Boil for 2 minutes or until liquid has almost evaporated. Stir in parsley and sugar. Season with salt and pepper. Remove from heat. Cover to keep warm.

2 Meanwhile, make Polenta Combine milk and stock in a large saucepan over high heat. Cover. Bring to the boil. Stir in polenta. Reduce heat to medium-low. Cook, stirring constantly, for 3 minutes or until polenta is thick. Stir in parmesan. Season with salt and pepper.

3 Serve mushroom mixture over polenta. Top with extra grated parmesan to serve.

NUTRITION: (per serve) 2044kJ; 21.6g fat; 13.1g sat fat; 19.9g protein; 43.3g carbs; 6.6g fibre; 62mg chol; 1162mg sodium.

COOK'S NOTE We used 200g each of Swiss browns, button and flat mushrooms.

High fibre

TURKISH EGGS

SERVES 4
PREP 5 minutes
COOK 15 minutes

1 tablespoon oil
1 large brown onion, halved, thinly sliced
2 teaspoons smoked paprika
2 x 410g cans tomato and paste with capsicum
4 eggs, at room temperature
4 rounds pita bread
½ cup roast garlic tzatziki

1 Preheat oven to 180°C/160°C fan-forced. Heat oil in a medium frying pan over medium-high heat. Add onion. Cook, stirring, for 5 minutes or until softened. Add paprika. Cook, stirring, for 1 minute or until fragrant. Add tomato and ¾ cup cold water. Season. Bring to a simmer.

2 Wrap pita bread in foil and place in oven. Cook for 5 minutes or until warm. Make 4 holes in tomato mixture. Crack 1 egg into each hole. Reduce heat to medium-low. Cook, covered, for 5 minutes or until eggs are cooked to your liking.

3 Serve with tzatziki and pita.

NUTRITION: (per serve) 1692kJ; 13.9g fat; 2.8g sat fat; 16.9g protein; 50.5g carbs; 5.8g fibre; 191mg chol; 600mg sodium.

High fibre, lower sodium, low saturated fat

INDONESIAN FRIED RICE

SERVES 4   **PREP** 5 minutes (plus cooling time)   **COOK** 15 minutes

1½ cups jasmine rice
1½ tablespoons peanut oil
4 green onions, thinly sliced
1 cup frozen peas
2 tablespoons sweet soy sauce
2 birdseye chillies, thinly sliced
4 eggs, at room temperature

1 Cook rice in a large saucepan of boiling water, following packet directions until tender. Drain. Spread rice on a tray to cool.

2 Heat a wok over high heat. Add 1 tablespoon oil to wok. Swirl to coat. Add ¾ onion. Stir-fry for 1 minute or until softened. Add peas. Stir-fry for 2 to 3 minutes or until bright green. Add cooled rice. Stir-fry for 3 minutes or until heated through.

3 Drizzle rice with sweet soy sauce. Add half the chilli. Season. Stir-fry for 2 minutes or until heated through. Remove from heat. Cover, keep warm.

4 Meanwhile, heat remaining oil in a large frying pan over medium heat. Crack eggs into pan. Cook for 2 minutes or until egg whites are set and yolks are still soft. Spoon rice into bowls. Top with a fried egg, remaining onion and chilli. Serve.

NUTRITION: (per serve) 1925kJ; 12.5g fat; 2.9g sat fat; 14.4g protein; 71g carbs; 3.4g fibre; 187mg chol; 532mg sodium.

Lower sodium, low saturated fat

VEGETARIAN PILAU

SERVES 4   **PREP** 5 minutes   **COOK** 20 minutes

⅓ cup slivered almonds
1½ tablespoons vegetable oil
1 large brown onion, finely chopped
400g frozen garden mix (see note)
1½ cups basmati rice
1 tablespoon garam masala
¾ cup roughly chopped fresh coriander leaves

1 Heat a large frying pan over medium heat. Add almonds. Cook, stirring, for 3 minutes or until golden. Transfer to a plate.

2 Heat oil in a large saucepan over medium heat. Add onion. Cook, stirring, for 3 minutes or until softened. Stir in vegetables, rice and garam masala. Cook for 1 minute or until fragrant. Stir in 2 cups cold water. Bring to the boil. Reduce heat to low. Cook, covered, for 15 minutes or until rice is tender and water has been absorbed.

3 Add half the almonds and coriander. Stir to combine. Spoon into bowls. Serve with remaining almonds and coriander.

NUTRITION: (per serve)1866kj; fat 13.6g; sat fat 1.4g; protein 10.2g; carbs 67.6g; fibre 6.1g; chol 0mg; sodium 40 mg.

COOK'S NOTE We used a frozen mix of carrot, broccoli, cauliflower, green beans and red capsicum.

Heart friendly, lower GI

ONION TARTE TATIN

SERVES 4
PREP 15 minutes
COOK 30 minutes

30g butter
¼ cup caster sugar
2 tablespoons white balsamic vinegar
2 medium white onions, cut into 5mm-thick rings (see note)
1 tablespoon fresh thyme leaves
375g block frozen puff pastry, partially thawed
Fresh thyme sprigs, to serve

1 Preheat oven to 220°C/200°C fan-forced.

2 Melt butter and sugar together in a 22cm-round (base), flameproof frying pan over medium heat. Cook, without stirring, for 5 minutes or until starting to turn golden. Stir in vinegar. Cook for 2 minutes. Arrange onion slices, side by side, in a single layer, in pan. Cook for 2 minutes or until onion starts to soften. Sprinkle with thyme leaves.

3 Meanwhile, on a lightly floured surface, roll pastry out until 3mm thick. Cut a 24cm round from pastry. Discard pastry scraps. Place pastry round over onion in pan, tucking in edge.

4 Bake for 15 to 18 minutes or until the pastry is golden and puffed (cover loosely with foil if it is over-browning during cooking). Stand in pan for 2 minutes. Carefully turn out onto a plate. Serve sprinkled with thyme sprigs.

NUTRITION: (per serve) 1595kJ; 18.5g fat; 10g sat fat; 5.1g protein; 47.9g carbs; 2.1g fibre; 38mg chol; 332mg sodium.

COOK'S NOTE Don't separate onion into rings, keep in thick slices.

Lower sodium

CURRIED VEGETABLE PILAF

SERVES 4
PREP 10 minutes
COOK 25 minutes

1 tablespoon vegetable oil
1 brown onion, thinly sliced
½ cup balti curry paste
1½ cups basmati rice
400ml can coconut milk
420g packet one-minute stir-fry vegetable mix
1 bunch fresh coriander, leaves picked

1 Heat oil in a large saucepan over medium-high heat. Add onion. Cook, stirring occasionally, for 5 minutes or until lightly browned. Add curry paste. Cook for 1 minute or until fragrant.

2 Stir in rice to coat. Add coconut milk and 1 cup cold water. Bring to the boil. Cover. Reduce heat to low. Cook for 15 minutes or until the liquid has been absorbed. Stir in vegetable mix. Set aside, covered, for 5 minutes to steam.

3 Stir in half the coriander. Divide between serving bowls. Sprinkle with remaining coriander. Serve.

NUTRITION: (per serve) 2917kJ; 36.6g fat; 19.6g sat fat; 12g protein; 77.2g carbs; 4.9g fibre; 0mg chol; 805mg sodium.

medium heat. Add onion. Cook, stirring, for 15 to 18 minutes or until golden and caramelised. Combine yoghurt and garlic in a small bowl. Season.

4 Fluff rice with fork. Add cauliflower mixture and coriander. Gently toss to combine. Transfer to large serving plate. Top with caramelised onion and coriander leaves. Serve with garlic yoghurt.

NUTRITION: (per serve) 2344kJ; 18.3g fat; 7.7g sat fat; 15.6g protein; 80.1g carbs; 5.2g fibre; 25mg chol; 1283mg sodium.

High fibre

SPINACH & DILL FRITTATA BURGER

SERVES 4   **PREP** 10 minutes   **COOK** 30 minutes

1 tablespoon olive oil
1 leek, trimmed, halved, washed, sliced
2 teaspoons ground cumin
50g baby spinach, shredded
6 eggs, lightly beaten
4 green onions, trimmed, sliced
¼ cup chopped fresh dill
1 teaspoon baking powder
Chargrilled Turkish bread, spicy tomato relish, lettuce
    and mayonnaise, to serve

1 Preheat oven to 200°C/180°C fan-forced. Grease a 6cm-deep, 20cm-square (base) cake pan. Line base and sides with baking paper, extending paper 3cm above edge of pan on all sides.

2 Heat oil in a medium frying pan over medium heat. Add leek. Cook, stirring, for 8 minutes or until soft. Add cumin and spinach. Stir for 1 minute or until spinach wilts. Transfer to a bowl.

3 Add egg, onion, dill and baking powder to spinach mixture. Season with salt and pepper. Stir to combine. Pour mixture into prepared pan. Bake for 15 to 20 minutes or until light golden and set. Stand 5 minutes. Lift from pan. Cut into quarters, then in half to form triangles. Serve frittata on Turkish bread with tomato relish, lettuce and mayonnaise.

NUTRITION: (per serve) 2013kJ; 29.8g fat; 5.1g sat fat; 16.5g protein; 35.7g carbs; 3.5g fibre; 304mg chol; 650mg sodium.

LEBANESE RICE WITH LENTILS & ROASTED CAULIFLOWER

SERVES 4   **PREP** 10 minutes   **COOK** 20 minutes

½ cauliflower, cut into florets
2 teaspoons sumac
1½ tablespoons olive oil
3 brown onions
1½ cups white long-grain rice
2½ cups vegetable stock
400g can lentils, drained, rinsed
20g butter
1 cup plain Greek-style yoghurt
1 garlic clove, crushed
½ cup roughly chopped fresh coriander leaves
Fresh coriander leaves, to serve

1 Preheat oven to 200°C/180°C fan-forced. Place cauliflower, sumac and 2 teaspoons oil in a roasting dish. Toss to coat. Season. Roast for 20 minutes or until golden and tender.

2 Meanwhile, finely chop 1 onion. Heat 2 teaspoons of oil in a large saucepan over medium-high heat. Add onion. Cook, stirring, for 5 minutes or until softened. Add rice. Stir. Add stock and lentils. Season. Bring to the boil. Cover. Reduce heat to low. Simmer for 12 to 15 minutes or until rice is tender.

3 Meanwhile, thinly slice remaining onions. Heat butter and remaining oil in a large frying pan over

VEGETABLE DONBURI

SERVES 4
PREP 10 minutes
COOK 20 minutes

1⅓ cups Japanese-style sushi rice
1 bunch broccolini, trimmed
150g button mushrooms, halved
1 large carrot, halved lengthways, sliced diagonally
1 tablespoon miso paste
2 tablespoons light soy sauce
1 tablespoon mirin seasoning
1 tablespoon caster sugar
6 eggs, lightly beaten
Sliced green onion, to serve

1 Cook rice following packet directions until tender. Cover to keep hot.

2 Meanwhile, cut broccolini stalks into 2cm pieces. Halve the florets. Pour 2 cups cold water into a medium, 8cm-deep frying pan. Bring to a simmer over medium heat. Add broccolini stalks, mushroom and carrot. Simmer for 5 minutes or until vegetables are tender. Add broccolini florets, miso paste, soy sauce, mirin seasoning and sugar. Simmer for 2 minutes or until vegetables are just tender (see note).

3 Pour egg over vegetable mixture. Simmer for 5 minutes or until cooked.

4 Divide rice between serving bowls. Using a large metal spoon, spoon egg mixture and broth over rice. Sprinkle with green onion. Serve.

NUTRITION: (per serve) 1776kJ; 8.4g fat; 2.4g sat fat; 18.5g protein; 66.6g carbs; 3.9g fibre; 281mg chol; 1076mg sodium.

COOK'S NOTE Don't drain the water from the frying pan as it becomes the broth for this dish.

Low kilojoule, low saturated fat

BROCCOLINI PAD THAI

SERVES 4
PREP 10 minutes
COOK 10 minutes

440g packet shelf-fresh Thai flat rice noodles
2 tablespoons peanut oil
1 brown onion, finely chopped
2 bunches broccolini, trimmed, cut into 3cm lengths
1 carrot, halved, thinly sliced diagonally
240g jar pad Thai paste
2 eggs, lightly beaten

1 Place noodles in a heatproof bowl. Cover with boiling water. Stand for 2 minutes. Gently separate noodles. Drain.

2 Heat a wok over high heat. Add oil. Swirl to coat. Add onion. Stir-fry for 1 minute or until tender. Add broccolini and carrot. Stir-fry for 4 minutes or until almost tender. Add paste. Stir-fry for 2 minutes or until fragrant.

3 Make a well in the centre of vegetables. Add egg. Cook for 1 minute or until set. Add noodles to wok. Stir-fry mixture for 1 to 2 minutes or until heated through, breaking up egg. Serve.

NUTRITION: (per serve) 1881kJ; 19.5g fat; 3.2g sat fat; 10.5g protein; 56.7g carbs; 3.4g fibre; 94mg chol; 1222mg sodium.

Low saturated fat

MUSHROOM & MIXED HERB OMELETTE

SERVES 2

PREP 10 minutes

COOK 18 minutes

40g butter

200g button mushrooms, sliced

1 garlic clove, crushed

2 teaspoons finely chopped fresh tarragon

2 tablespoons finely chopped fresh flat-leaf parsley leaves

1 teaspoon finely grated lemon rind

4 eggs

50g fresh ricotta, crumbled

1 Melt 20g butter in a 19cm (base) non-stick frying pan over medium heat. Add mushrooms. Cook for 2 to 3 minutes or until just tender. Add garlic, tarragon, parsley and lemon rind. Cook for 1 minute or until fragrant. Transfer to a bowl. Cover to keep warm. Wipe pan clean.

2 Whisk eggs in a bowl. Melt half the remaining butter in pan over medium-high heat until hot. Reduce heat to medium-low. Add half the egg, tilting pan so egg covers base. Cook for 3 to 4 minutes or until egg is set and underside golden.

3 Sprinkle half the ricotta over half of the omelette. Using a slotted spoon, spoon half the mushroom mixture over ricotta. Season with salt and pepper. Fold omelette over filling. Slide omelette onto a plate. Repeat with remaining ingredients. Serve.

NUTRITION: (per serve) 1505kJ; 29.7g fat; 15.7g sat fat; 19.5g protein; 2.8g carbs; 3.5g fibre; 438mg chol; 433mg sodium.

Gluten free, lower sodium

ZUCCHINI & PUMPKIN FRITTERS WITH POACHED EGGS

SERVES 4
PREP 10 minutes
COOK 18 minutes

2 zucchini, grated
400g butternut pumpkin, peeled, grated
½ cup plain flour
1 teaspoon baking powder
¼ cup chopped fresh coriander leaves
5 eggs
Vegetable oil, for shallow frying
1 tablespoon white vinegar
1 teaspoon salt
400g tomato medley (see note)
1 tablespoon chopped fresh chives
1 tablespoon olive oil

1 Squeeze excess moisture from zucchini and pumpkin. Place zucchini and pumpkin in a bowl. Add flour, baking powder, coriander and 1 egg. Season with salt and pepper. Mix well to combine.

2 Add enough vegetable oil to a deep frying pan to come 5mm up side of pan. Heat over medium heat. Spoon ¼ cup of zucchini mixture into pan, spreading slightly with a spatula. Repeat to make 3 more rounds. Cook for 2 to 3 minutes each side or until browned. Transfer to a plate lined with paper towel to drain. Cover, to keep warm. Repeat with remaining mixture to make a total of 16 fritters.

3 Meanwhile, fill a medium saucepan with cold water until 8cm deep. Add 2 teaspoons white vinegar and salt. Bring to the boil over high heat. Reduce heat to low (water should still be simmering at edge). Crack 1 of the remaining eggs into a small bowl. Using a wooden spoon, stir water to create a whirlpool. Tip egg into water. Cook for 3 to 4 minutes or until white is set and yolk is still soft. Using a slotted spoon, remove egg from water and transfer to a plate. Using a large metal spoon, skim foam from water. Repeat with remaining eggs.

4 Combine tomatoes, chives, olive oil and remaining vinegar in a bowl. Season with salt and pepper. Serve fritters with salad and poached eggs.

NUTRITION: (per serve) 1616kJ; 25.9g fat; 4.4g sat fat; 12.2g protein; 26g carbs; 5.2g fibre; 234mg chol; 973mg sodium.

COOK'S NOTE Quarter the larger tomatoes and halve the medium ones.

High fibre, low kilojoule, low saturated fat

GAZPACHO WITH SMOKY PEPITAS

SERVES 4

PREP 20 minutes

COOK 7 minutes

2 tablespoons pumpkin seeds (pepitas)

Olive oil cooking spray

¼ teaspoon smoked paprika

1kg ripe tomatoes, chopped

2 large yellow capsicums, chopped

½ cup fresh basil leaves

2 tablespoons red wine vinegar

2 tablespoons olive oil

75g fetta, crumbled

Buttered light rye toast and small fresh basil leaves, to serve

1 Preheat oven to 200°C/180°C fan-forced. Line a baking tray with baking paper. Place pepitas on prepared tray. Spray with oil. Sprinkle with paprika. Toss to coat. Bake for 5 to 7 minutes or until toasted.

2 Meanwhile, place tomato, capsicum, basil, vinegar and oil in a food processor. Process until almost smooth and combined.

3 Divide soup between bowls. Top with pepitas, fetta and basil leaves. Serve with rye toast.

NUTRITION: (per serve) 1536kJ; 21g fat; 6.7g sat fat; 12.5g protein; 28.1g carbs; 7.3g fibre; 22mg chol; 477mg sodium.

High fibre, lower sodium, low kilojoule

AVOCADO PANZANELLA SALAD

SERVES 6 (as a side)
PREP 20 minutes
COOK 5 minutes

½ x 450g ciabatta loaf, cut into 2.5cm cubes
¼ cup extra virgin olive oil
400g punnet tomato medley, halved
½ red onion, thinly sliced
1 Lebanese cucumber, halved, thickly sliced
180g fetta, cut into 2cm pieces
1 cup fresh basil leaves, torn
1 cup mixed pitted olives, sliced
2 avocados, halved, cut into 3cm pieces
¼ cup red wine vinegar
½ cup fresh flat-leaf parsley leaves

1 Preheat grill on high. Place bread on a baking tray. Drizzle with 1 tablespoon oil. Season with salt and pepper. Turn to coat. Cook under grill for 2 to 3 minutes, turning, or until golden. Set aside to cool.

2 Place tomato, onion, cucumber, fetta, basil, olives, avocado and bread in a large bowl. Gently toss to combine. Place vinegar and remaining oil in a screw-top jar. Season with salt and pepper. Secure lid. Shake well to combine.

3 Transfer salad to a large shallow serving bowl. Sprinkle with parsley. Drizzle with dressing. Serve.

NUTRITION: (per serve) 1838kJ; 32.7g fat; 9.5g sat fat; 10.5g protein; 24.4g carbs; 3.8g fibre; 20mg chol; 753mg sodium.

High fibre

VEGETARIAN NACHOS WITH GUACAMOLE

SERVES 4
PREP 15 minutes
COOK 15 minutes

175g packet original corn chips
435g can refried beans
1 cup grated 4 cheese blend
½ cup thick and chunky salsa
Light sour cream and fresh coriander leaves, to serve
Guacamole
2 medium avocados, chopped
1 medium tomato, seeded, finely chopped
2 teaspoons lime juice
1 tablespoon finely chopped fresh coriander leaves

1 Preheat oven to 200°C/180°C fan-forced. Spread corn chips over base of a 6 cup-capacity baking dish. Dollop beans over chips. Sprinkle with cheese. Bake for 15 minutes, or until cheese has melted.

2 Meanwhile, make Guacamole Place avocado in a bowl. Mash with a fork until smooth. Stir in tomato, lime juice and coriander. Season with salt and pepper. Serve nachos topped with salsa, guacamole, sour cream and coriander leaves.

NUTRITION: (per serve) 2382kj; fat 36.2g; sat fat 13.4g; protein 13.9g; carbs 43.3g; fibre 10.1g; chol 18mg; sodium 970 mg.

FALAFEL FATTOUSH

SERVES 4
PREP 20 minutes
COOK 10 minutes

⅓ cup rice bran oil
2 small rounds Lebanese bread, split, torn into 3cm pieces
200g packet falafel mix
¼ teaspoon mild chilli powder
250g cherry tomatoes, halved
1 Lebanese cucumber, seeded, thickly sliced
1 green capsicum, chopped
1 small red onion, cut into thin wedges
4 radishes, trimmed, thinly sliced
1 cup loosely packed fresh flat-leaf parsley leaves
1 cup loosely packed fresh mint leaves
Hummus dressing
125g tub hummus
2 tablespoons lemon juice
1 tablespoon extra virgin olive oil

1 Pour oil into a medium frying pan over medium-high heat. Cook bread, in batches, for 1 minute or until golden and crisp. Transfer to a baking tray lined with paper towel to drain. Cool.

2 Make falafel mixture following packet directions. Stir in chilli powder. Season with salt and pepper. Shape mixture into 16 patties (approx 1 tablespoon per patty). Add more oil to pan if necessary. Cook falafel, in batches, for 1 to 2 minutes each side or until browned. Transfer to a baking tray lined with paper towel to drain.

3 Make Hummus dressing Combine ingredients in a small bowl. Season with salt and pepper.

4 Arrange bread, tomato, cucumber, capsicum, onion, radish, parsley, mint and falafel on a platter. Season with pepper. Drizzle with dressing. Serve.

NUTRITION: (per serve) 2390kJ; 26.7g fat; 5.1g sat fat; 17.7g protein; 64.6g carbs; 8.4g fibre; 0mg chol; 850mg sodium.

High fibre, low saturated fat

ZUCCHINI, RICOTTA & PUMPKIN TARTS

SERVES 4
PREP 15 minutes
COOK 25 minutes

500g butternut pumpkin, peeled, cut into 1.5cm
   pieces
2 medium zucchini, cut into ribbons
250g fresh ricotta, crumbled
2 tablespoons chopped fresh chives
2 sheets frozen puff pastry, partially thawed
1 egg, lightly beaten
Extra chopped fresh chives, mixed salad leaves and
   lemon wedges, to serve

1 Preheat oven to 220°C/200°C fan-forced. Line a baking tray with baking paper.

2 Place pumpkin in a heatproof, microwave-safe bowl. Add 2 tablespoons cold water. Cover with plastic wrap. Microwave on HIGH (100%) for 3 minutes or until tender. Drain. Add zucchini. Stir to combine.

3 Combine 200g ricotta and chives in a bowl. Season with salt and pepper.

4 Cut pastry sheets in half to form 4 rectangles. Place on prepared tray. Starting with the short sides first, fold 1cm of pastry edges inwards to create a border. Spread inside border of each tart with ¼ cup ricotta mixture. Top with pumpkin mixture. Season with salt and pepper. Brush edges with egg. Bake for 20 minutes until pastry is golden and puffed.

5 Sprinkle tarts with remaining ricotta and extra chives. Serve tarts with salad and lemon wedges.

NUTRITION: (per serve) 1832kJ; 21.4g fat; 11.2g sat fat; 13g protein; 47.8g carbs; 5.4g fibre; 74mg chol; 565mg sodium.

High fibre, lower sodium

CHICKEN

HOISIN CHICKEN STIR-FRY

SERVES 4   **PREP** 15 minutes   **COOK** 10 minutes

450g fresh wide rice noodles
1 tablespoon peanut oil
1 medium red capsicum, chopped
1 large carrot, halved lengthways, thinly sliced
150g sugar snap peas, trimmed
2 garlic cloves, crushed
2 green onions, thinly sliced
1 long red chilli, thinly sliced
2½ cups cooked, sliced chicken
¼ cup hoisin sauce
2 tablespoons soy sauce

1 Place noodles in a large heatproof bowl. Cover with boiling water. Stand for 3 to 4 minutes or until tender. Using a fork, separate noodles. Drain.

2 Meanwhile, heat a wok over high heat. Add oil. Swirl to coat. Add capsicum and carrot. Stir-fry for 3 minutes or until softened. Add peas, garlic, onion and chilli. Stir-fry for 2 minutes or until just tender.

3 Add chicken and sauces. Season. Stir-fry for 2 minutes or until heated. Add noodles. Toss for 1 to 2 minutes or until hot. Serve.

NUTRITION: (per serve) 2479kJ; 21.9g fat; 4.9g sat fat; 35.8g protein; 59.2g carbs; 6.6g fibre; 130mg chol; 1092mg sodium.

Low saturated fat, high fibre, lower GI

CORONATION CHICKEN & MANGO SALAD

SERVES 4   **PREP** 20 minutes   **COOK** 15 minutes

2 tablespoons olive oil
3cm piece fresh ginger, finely grated
1 tablespoon mild curry powder
½ cup mango and ginger chutney (see note)
¼ cup dried apricots, thinly sliced
½ cup mayonnaise
2 teaspoons worcestershire sauce
4 chicken breast fillets
1 large mango, thinly sliced
1 green oakleaf lettuce, leaves separated
1 Lebanese cucumber, cut into ribbons
⅓ cup roughly chopped fresh coriander
¼ cup flaked almonds, toasted
Lime wedges, to serve

1 Heat half the oil in a small saucepan over medium heat. Cook ginger and curry powder, stirring, for 1 minute or until fragrant. Transfer to a large bowl. Stir in chutney, apricots, mayonnaise and sauce.

2 Cut each chicken fillet in half lengthways to form 2 thin fillets.

3 Heat a barbecue hotplate or chargrill over medium-high heat. Brush chicken with remaining oil. Season with salt and pepper. Cook chicken, in batches, for 2 to 3 minutes each side or until browned and cooked through. Transfer to a chopping board. Slice thickly.

4 Add chicken and mango to mayonnaise mixture. Toss gently to combine. Spoon chicken mixture onto lettuce and cucumber. Sprinkle with coriander and almonds. Serve with lime wedges.

NUTRITION: (per serve) 2709kJ; 38.5g fat; 5.5g sat fat; 36.4g protein; 36.9g carbs; 4.4g fibre; 108mg chol; 747mg sodium.

COOK'S NOTE You can find mango and ginger chutney in the Indian section of your local supermarket.

CHICKEN, CHICKPEA & FETTA SALAD

SERVES 4

PREP 15 minutes

1 large barbecue chicken

400g can chickpeas, drained, rinsed

285g jar whole piquillo peppers, drained, rinsed, thinly sliced (see note)

350g jar marinated fetta

2½ tablespoons red wine vinegar

100g baby rocket

1 Remove and discard skin and bones from chicken. Shred chicken. Combine chicken, chickpeas and peppers in a large bowl.

2 Drain fetta, reserving ½ cup oil. Combine reserved oil and vinegar in a small jug. Add to chicken mixture. Toss to combine.

3 Add rocket and fetta. Toss to combine. Serve.

NUTRITION: (per serve) 2487kJ; 37.6g fat; 19.5g sat fat; 49.1g protein; 13.5g carbs; 3.8g fibre; 110mg chol; 1305mg sodium.

COOK'S NOTE Piquillo peppers are a Spanish variety of chilli. You can use chargrilled capsicum instead of the peppers.

CHICKEN 'NACHOS' SALAD

SERVES 4

PREP 15 minutes

250g light sour cream

1 large barbecue chicken

230g packet corn chips

1 avocado, diced

1 cup enchilada sauce

1 cup small fresh coriander sprigs

1 Place sour cream and 2 tablespoons warm water in a small bowl. Stir until smooth and combined.

2 Meanwhile, remove and discard skin and bones from chicken. Thickly shred chicken.

3 Place a layer of corn chips on a serving platter or dish. Arrange ⅓ of chicken, sour cream mixture, avocado, sauce and a few coriander sprigs on platter. Repeat layering with remaining ingredients and finishing with coriander sprigs. Serve.

NUTRITION: (per serve) 3029kJ; 42.4g fat; 16g sat fat; 39g protein; 45.5g carbs; 4.1g fibre; 146mg chol; 802mg sodium.

WARM CHICKEN & LENTIL SALAD

SERVES 4   **PREP** 20 minutes   **COOK** 10 minutes

1 large barbecue chicken
2 tablespoons extra virgin olive oil
2 garlic cloves, finely chopped
250g baby roma tomatoes, halved
2 x 400g cans lentils, drained, rinsed
2 tablespoons white balsamic dressing
100g baby spinach

1 Remove and discard skin and bones from chicken. Thickly shred chicken, then chop.

2 Heat oil in a large frying pan over medium-high heat. Add garlic. Cook for 2 minutes or until fragrant. Add chicken and tomatoes. Cook, stirring, for 3 minutes or until warmed through.

3 Add lentils and dressing. Toss gently for 1 to 2 minutes or until heated through and well combined. Serve chicken mixture on spinach. Season with pepper. Serve.

NUTRITION: (per serve) 1713kJ; 22.6g fat; 4.2g sat fat; 36.8g protein; 12g carbs; 5.6g fibre; 106mg chol; 625mg sodium.

High fibre, low kilojoule, low saturated fat

CHICKEN & MUSHROOM FRITTATA

SERVES 4   **PREP** 10 minutes   **COOK** 25 minutes

2 teaspoons olive oil
500g chicken and mushroom sausages
200g button mushrooms, quartered
2 green onions, trimmed, thinly sliced
8 eggs, lightly beaten
150g grape tomatoes, halved
100g fetta, crumbled

1 Heat oil in a 2.5cm-deep, 20cm x 26cm (10 cup-capacity) heavy-based, flameproof dish. Cook sausages, turning, for 8 to 10 minutes or until browned and just cooked through. Transfer to a plate. Slice thickly.

2 Add mushroom to dish. Cook for 4 to 5 minutes or until softened. Return sausages with onion to dish. Toss well to combine. Pour egg over sausage mixture. Top with tomato and fetta. Reduce heat to low. Cook for 5 minutes or until almost set.

3 Meanwhile, preheat grill on medium. Grill frittata for 5 to 6 minutes or until lightly browned and centre is firm to touch. Serve.

NUTRITION: (per serve) 2109kJ; 35.5g fat; 13.2g sat fat; 35.9g protein; 9.6g carbs; 2g fibre; 454mg chol; 1614mg sodium.

cucumber in a bowl. Drizzle over soy sauce mixture. Gently toss to combine. Serve.

NUTRITION: (per serve) 2194kJ; 4.8g fat; 1.2g sat fat; 37.2g protein; 79.7g carbs; 3.6g fibre; 85mg chol; 560mg sodium.

Lower sodium, low saturated fat

MANGO & COCONUT CHICKEN SKEWERS

SERVES 4   **PREP** 10 minutes   **COOK** 20 minutes
You'll need 8 pre-soaked bamboo skewers
800g chicken thigh fillets, trimmed, cut into 3cm
   pieces
½ cup mango chutney
1 tablespoon crunchy peanut butter
1 tablespoon soy sauce
270ml can light coconut cream
100g Asian salad leaf mix
3 radishes, thinly sliced
1 Lebanese cucumber, peeled, thinly sliced
2 teaspoons Asian salad dressing

1 Thread chicken evenly onto 8 skewers. Combine chutney, peanut butter and soy sauce in a bowl. Transfer 2 tablespoons mixture to a small bowl. Brush mixture over chicken skewers. Reserve remaining mixture.

2 Heat a well-oiled barbecue or chargrill pan over medium heat. Cook skewers, in batches, for 3 to 4 minutes each side or until browned and cooked through.

3 Meanwhile, place coconut cream and reserved mango chutney mixture in a small saucepan over medium heat. Cook, stirring, for 6 to 8 minutes or until reduced by half and mixture has thickened slightly.

4 Place salad mix, radish, cucumber and dressing in a bowl. Toss to combine. Place skewers on a platter. Drizzle with a little coconut mixture. Serve with salad and remaining coconut mixture.

NUTRITION: (per serve) 1963kJ; 25.7g fat; 12.8g sat fat; 38.6g protein; 20.6g carbs; 2.2g fibre; 165mg chol; 854mg sodium.

SPICY SESAME CHICKEN NOODLE SALAD

SERVES 4   **PREP** 15 minutes   **COOK** 10 minutes
4 green onions, trimmed
2 (200g each) chicken breast fillets
440g thin egg-style noodles
½ teaspoon sichuan peppercorns
1½ tablespoons light soy sauce
1½ teaspoons sesame oil
1 teaspoon dried chilli flakes
1 Lebanese cucumber, halved lengthways, thinly
   sliced diagonally

1 Cut 2 green onions into 4cm-long pieces. Place onion and chicken in a medium saucepan. Cover with cold water. Bring to the boil over medium-high heat. Reduce heat to low. Simmer, covered, for 4 minutes or until chicken is just cooked through. Remove from heat. Stand chicken in cooking liquid for 6 minutes. Drain. Discard green onion.

2 When cool enough to handle, shred chicken. Place noodles in a large heatproof bowl. Cover with cold water. Using a fork, separate noodles. Drain well. Thinly slice remaining green onion. Using a mortar and pestle pound sichuan peppercorns.

3 Combine soy sauce, oil, chilli flakes and sichuan pepper in small bowl. Place chicken, onion and

PAD THAI RICE

SERVES 4
PREP 25 minutes
COOK 15 minutes

1⅓ cups jasmine rice
¼ cup lime juice
2 tablespoons fish sauce
2 tablespoons grated palm sugar
¼ cup peanut oil
200g chicken breast fillet, thinly sliced
300g firm tofu, cut into 2cm cubes
1 brown onion, halved, cut into thin wedges
2 garlic cloves, crushed
1 long red chilli, finely chopped
1 large carrot, halved lengthways, thinly sliced
200g green beans, trimmed, cut into 3cm lengths
2 eggs, lightly beaten
½ cup bean sprouts, trimmed
¼ cup fresh coriander leaves
Chopped roasted peanuts, sliced red chilli and lime wedges, to serve

1 Cook rice following absorption method on packet. Place lime juice, fish sauce and sugar in a bowl. Stir until sugar has dissolved.

2 Heat a wok over medium-high heat. Add 1 tablespoon oil. Swirl to coat. Add chicken. Stir-fry for 2 minutes or until browned. Transfer to a bowl. Add 1 tablespoon oil to wok. Swirl to coat. Add tofu. Stir-fry for 3 to 4 minutes or until golden. Transfer to a bowl.

3 Add remaining oil to wok. Add onion, garlic and chilli. Stir-fry for 2 minutes or until onion has softened. Add carrot and beans. Stir-fry for 3 minutes or until just tender. Make a well in centre of vegetables. Add egg. Cook, stirring occasionally, for 1 minute or until set. Roughly break into pieces.

4 Add rice, tofu, chicken and sauce mixture. Stir-fry for 2 minutes or until heated through. Add sprouts and coriander. Toss to combine. Divide between bowls. Top with peanuts and chilli and serve with lime wedges.

NUTRITION: (per serve) 2669kJ; 25.5g fat; 4.9g sat fat; 30.4g protein; 69.2g carbs; 6.6g fibre; 126mg chol; 1040mg sodium.

High fibre, low saturated fat

mint, coriander, onion and chilli, if using. Serve with lime wedges.

NUTRITION: (per serve) 1178kJ; 5.7g fat; 1.7g sat fat; 25.2g protein; 30.4g carbs; 1.4g fibre; 61mg chol; 1390mg sodium.

Low kilojoule, low saturated fat

OH-SO-EASY CHICKEN & LEEK 'PIES'

MAKES 6   **PREP** 15 minutes   **COOK** 25 minutes
1 tablespoon olive oil
600g chicken thigh fillets, trimmed, thinly sliced
4 rashers shortcut bacon, sliced
1 medium leek, trimmed, halved, washed, sliced
2 garlic cloves, crushed
2 teaspoons fresh rosemary leaves
¼ cup dry white wine
1½ sheets frozen puff pastry, partially thawed
1 egg, lightly beaten
2 teaspoons cornflour
½ cup chicken stock
¾ cup light thickened cooking cream
200g broccoli, finely chopped

1 Preheat oven to 220°C/200°C fan-forced. Heat oil in a large, deep frying pan over medium-high heat. Add chicken. Cook, stirring, for 5 minutes or until browned. Add bacon, leek, garlic and rosemary. Cook, stirring, for 5 minutes or until leek has softened. Add wine. Bring to the boil.

2 Meanwhile, line a baking tray with baking paper. Using an 8cm round cutter, cut 6 rounds from pastry. Place pastry rounds on prepared tray. Make shapes with pastry trimmings to decorate pastry rounds. Brush pastry with egg. Bake for 10 minutes or until pastry is golden and puffed.

3 Place cornflour in a jug. Add 2 tablespoons stock. Stir until smooth. Stir in remaining stock. Add stock mixture and cream to pan. Bring to the boil. Reduce heat to medium. Add broccoli. Simmer for 5 minutes or until chicken is cooked through and sauce has thickened. Season with salt and pepper. Spoon chicken mixture into 6 dishes. Top with pastry rounds. Serve.

NUTRITION: (per serve)1875kj; fat 27.1g; sat fat 11.2g; protein 28g; carbs 20.2g; fibre 3g; chol 154mg; sodium 635mg.

VIETNAMESE CHICKEN PHO

SERVES 4   **PREP** 20 minutes   **COOK** 15 minutes
1 litre salt-reduced chicken stock
4cm piece fresh ginger, peeled, halved
2 star anise
3 teaspoons light soy sauce
1 tablespoon fish sauce
½ x 250g packet Thai-style rice noodles
2 tablespoons lime juice
2 cups sliced cooked chicken breast
½ cup fresh mint leaves
½ cup fresh coriander leaves
2 green onions, thinly sliced
Thinly sliced red birdseye chilli, to serve

1 Combine stock, 2½ cups cold water, ginger, star anise, soy sauce and fish sauce in a large saucepan over high heat. Cover. Bring to the boil. Reduce heat to low. Simmer for 10 minutes.

2 Meanwhile, place noodles in a heatproof bowl. Cover with boiling water. Stand for 5 minutes or until tender. Separate noodles with a fork. Drain well.

3 Using a slotted spoon, remove star anise and ginger from stock mixture. Stir in lime juice. Divide noodles between serving bowls. Top with chicken. Pour over stock mixture. Sprinkle with

CHICKEN CAESAR SALAD

SERVES 4
PREP 30 minutes
COOK 12 minutes

1 small baguette, thinly sliced
Olive oil cooking spray
4 middle bacon rashers, trimmed, chopped
1 baby cos lettuce, leaves separated, torn
4 cups shredded cooked chicken
½ cup shaved parmesan
2 medium-boiled eggs, quartered

Caesar dressing
½ cup low-fat yoghurt
2 tablespoons low-fat mayonnaise
2 teaspoons wholegrain mustard

1 Preheat oven to 220°C/200°C fan-forced. Line a large baking tray with baking paper. Place bread, in a single layer, on tray. Spray with oil. Bake for 5 to 7 minutes, turning halfway, or until golden and crisp.

2 Make Caesar dressing Combine yoghurt, mayonnaise, mustard and 2 teaspoons warm water in a small bowl. Season.

3 Heat a non-stick frying pan over high heat. Add bacon. Cook, stirring, for 3 to 4 minutes or until crisp. Transfer to a plate lined with paper towel.

4 Place lettuce in a large bowl. Add croutons, bacon, chicken and parmesan. Toss to combine. Transfer to plates. Top with egg. Serve drizzled with dressing.

NUTRITION: (per serve) 2272kJ; 21.5g fat; 7.2g sat fat; 55.5g protein; 30.9g carbs; 2.2g fibre; 257mg chol; 1372mg sodium.

EASY CHICKEN FRIED RICE

SERVES 4
PREP 10 minutes
COOK 10 minutes

1½ cups long grain white rice
1 tablespoon vegetable oil
2 eggs, lightly beaten
2 cups diced frozen vegetable mix
1½ cups shredded cooked chicken
2 medium tomatoes, chopped
2 tablespoons gluten-free soy sauce

1 Cook rice in a large saucepan of boiling water, following packet directions until tender. Drain. Spread rice on a tray to cool.

2 Heat a wok over medium-high heat. Add half the oil. Swirl to coat. Add egg. Swirl to cover base of wok. Cook for 1 minute or until just set. Transfer to a board. Roughly chop egg.

3 Add remaining oil to wok. Swirl to coat. Stir-fry vegetable mix for 2 minutes. Add rice, chicken and tomato. Stir-fry for 3 to 4 minutes or until rice is heated through. Add soy sauce. Stir-fry for 1 minute. Stir through egg. Season with pepper. Serve.

NUTRITION: (per serve) 1979kJ; 11.7g fat; 2.6g sat fat; 24g protein; 65.1g carbs; 3.7g fibre; 141mg chol; 748mg sodium.

Gluten free, low saturated fat

RICE NOODLE, CHICKEN & PINEAPPLE SALAD

SERVES 4
PREP 20 minutes
100g dried rice vermicelli noodles
1 large barbecue chicken
650g fresh pineapple, peeled, cored, diced
1 small iceberg lettuce, cored, thinly shredded
1 cup fresh mint leaves, shredded
¾ cup Thai dressing
Extra mint leaves, to serve

1 Place noodles in a heatproof bowl. Cover with boiling water. Set aside for 10 minutes or until just softened. Drain.

2 Meanwhile, remove and discard skin and bones from chicken. Shred chicken.

3 Place noodles, chicken, pineapple, lettuce, mint and dressing in a large bowl. Using tongs, toss until well combined. Serve with extra mint leaves.

NUTRITION: (per serve) 1594kJ; 11.6g fat; 3g sat fat; 33.5g protein; 33.2g carbs; 4.6g fibre; 106mg chol; 501mg sodium.

Low kilojoule, lower sodium, low saturated fat

WARM CHICKEN & BOCCONCINI SALAD

SERVES 4
PREP 10 minutes (plus standing time)
COOK 12 minutes
2 (400g) chicken breast fillets
1½ tablespoons extra virgin olive oil
100g baby spinach leaves
220g tub baby bocconcini cheese, drained, halved
¼ cup pine nuts, toasted
1 large avocado, sliced
2 tablespoons balsamic vinegar

1 Drizzle chicken with 2 teaspoons oil. Season with salt and pepper. Heat a chargrill pan over medium-high heat. Cook chicken for 5 to 6 minutes each side or until browned and cooked through. Transfer to a plate. Cover. Stand for 5 minutes. Thinly slice chicken.

2 Place spinach, cheese, pine nuts, avocado and chicken in a bowl. Place vinegar and remaining oil in a screw-top jar. Season with salt and pepper. Secure lid. Shake well to combine.

3 Drizzle dressing over salad. Toss gently to combine. Serve.

NUTRITION: (per serve) 2315kJ; 44.3g fat; 11.8g sat fat; 35.1g protein; 4.1g carbs; 2.6g fibre; 84mg chol; 288mg sodium.

Lower sodium, gluten free

CHICKEN, BROCCOLI & DUKKAH SALAD

SERVES 4
PREP 10 minutes
COOK 15 minutes

2½ tablespoons olive oil
2 small (500g total) chicken breast fillets
500g broccoli, cut into florets
2 teaspoons finely grated lemon rind
1 tablespoon lemon juice
⅓ cup pine nuts
¼ cup pistachio dukkah (see note)
120g baby spinach

1 Heat 2 teaspoons oil in a large, deep frying pan over medium-high heat. Cook chicken for 4 to 5 minutes each side or until cooked through. Transfer to a plate. Cover with foil. Stand for 5 minutes. Slice. Wipe pan.

2 Meanwhile, place broccoli in a large, heatproof microwave-safe bowl. Add 2 tablespoons cold water. Cover with plastic wrap. Microwave on HIGH (100%) for 2 minutes or until bright green and tender.

3 Combine lemon rind, lemon juice and remaining oil in a bowl.

4 Place pine nuts in frying pan over medium heat. Cook, tossing, for 2 minutes or until toasted. Transfer to a bowl. Add dukkah to pan. Cook, stirring, for 1 minute or until fragrant. Add chicken, broccoli and pine nuts to pan. Toss for 1 to 2 minutes or until coated. Transfer to a heatproof bowl.

5 Add spinach and dressing to chicken and season. Toss to combine. Serve.

NUTRITION: (per serve) 1920kJ; 29.8g fat; 3.7g sat fat; 38.8g protein; 5.6g carbs; 7g fibre; 81mg chol; 250mg sodium.

COOK'S NOTE Dukkah is a blend of nuts, sesame seeds, herbs and spices. It is found in the spice aisle.

High fibre, low kilojoule, heart friendly

STICKY CHICKEN DRUMETTES WITH GRILLED CORN & ROCKET SALAD

SERVES 4   **PREP** 5 minutes   **COOK** 25 minutes

⅓ cup plum sauce
2 garlic cloves, crushed
1½ tablespoons worcestershire sauce
1kg chicken drumettes
Grilled corn and rocket salad
4 corn cobs, husks and silk removed
Olive oil cooking spray
250g cherry tomatoes, quartered
60g baby rocket
2 tablespoons lemon juice
1 tablespoon olive oil

1 Preheat the oven to 200°C/180°C fan-forced. Line a large baking tray with baking paper.

2 Combine plum sauce, garlic, worcestershire and 1 tablespoon cold water in a large bowl. Add chicken. Toss to coat. Place on prepared tray. Bake for 25 minutes or until browned and cooked through.

3 Meanwhile, make Grilled corn and rocket salad Preheat barbecue chargrill on high. Spray corn with oil. Cook, turning, for 6 to 8 minutes or until browned and tender. Transfer to a board. Cool for 5 minutes. Using a sharp knife, cut kernels off corn cobs and transfer to a bowl. Add tomato, rocket, lemon juice and oil. Season with salt and pepper. Toss to combine.

4 Serve chicken with salad.

NUTRITION: (per serve) 2426kJ; 32.7g fat; 8.6g sat fat; 30g protein; 37.7g carbs; 7.6g fibre; 87mg chol; 285mg sodium.

High fibre, lower sodium

TROPICAL CHICKEN BURGERS

SERVES 4   **PREP** 15 minutes   **COOK** 10 minutes

500g chicken mince
1 cup fresh breadcrumbs
1 egg, lightly beaten
2 green onions, finely chopped
¼ cup smoky barbecue sauce
4 shortcut bacon rashers
4 x 1cm-thick slices fresh pineapple, peeled, core removed
4 hamburger buns, halved
Olive oil cooking spray
¼ cup whole-egg mayonnaise
4 butter lettuce leaves
100g cheddar cheese, thinly sliced

1 Combine mince, breadcrumbs, egg, onion and 1 tablespoon sauce in a large bowl. Shape mixture into four 2cm-thick patties. Heat a greased barbecue plate and chargrill on medium-high. Cook patties on plate for 4 to 5 minutes each side or until cooked.

2 Meanwhile, cook bacon and pineapple with patties on barbecue plate for 1 to 2 minutes each side or until browned. Spray cut sides of buns with oil. Cook on chargrill for 2 minutes each side or until browned.

3 Spread bun bases with mayonnaise. Top with lettuce, pineapple, patties, cheese and bacon. Drizzle with remaining barbecue sauce. Sandwich with bun tops.

NUTRITION: (per serve) 3126kJ; 30.5g fat; 11.3g sat fat; 48.8g protein; 64.7g carbs; 4.2g fibre; 163mg chol; 1398mg sodium.

TANDOORI CHICKEN & MANGO SALAD WITH LIME DRESSING

SERVES 4

PREP 15 minutes

COOK 15 minutes

⅓ cup tandoori paste

¼ cup plain Greek-style yoghurt

600g chicken breast fillets

1 large mango, thinly sliced

1 Lebanese cucumber, halved, thinly sliced

1 small red onion, cut into thin wedges

1 cup fresh mint leaves

80g baby spinach

1 lime, peeled, white pith removed, flesh finely
    chopped

2 tablespoons extra virgin olive oil

Warm naan bread, to serve (see note)

1 Preheat oven to 200°C/180°C fan-forced. Line a large baking tray with baking paper.

2 Combine paste and yoghurt in a medium bowl. Season with salt and pepper. Add chicken. Turn to coat.

3 Place chicken on prepared tray. Bake for 15 minutes or until browned and cooked through. Remove from oven. Cover loosely with foil. Stand for 5 minutes. Thickly slice.

4 Combine mango, cucumber, onion, mint, spinach and half the chicken in a large bowl. Whisk lime and oil in a small bowl. Season with salt and pepper. Add to salad. Toss to coat. Place salad on a platter. Top with remaining chicken. Serve with naan bread.

NUTRITION: (per serve) 2123kJ; 17.4g fat; 5.1g sat fat; 41.3g protein; 43g carbs; 5.7g fibre; 103mg chol; 1275mg sodium.

COOK'S NOTE Wrap naan in foil and bake in the last 5 minutes of cooking.

High fibre, low saturated fat

NO-FUSS CHICKEN GOULASH

SERVES 4   **PREP** 10 minutes   **COOK** 30 minutes

1 tablespoon olive oil
6 chicken thigh fillets, chopped
1 brown onion, halved, thickly sliced
250g button mushrooms, halved
1 red capsicum, chopped
2 garlic cloves, crushed
1 tablespoon sweet paprika
2 tablespoons no-added salt tomato paste
400g can cherry tomatoes in juice
300g dried fettuccine
2 tablespoons light sour cream
2 tablespoons chopped fresh chives

1 Heat 2 teaspoons oil in a large saucepan on medium-high heat. Cook chicken, stirring, for 2 to 3 minutes or until browned. Transfer to a bowl.

2 Reduce heat to medium. Heat remaining oil in pan. Add onion, mushroom, capsicum, garlic and paprika. Cook for 5 minutes or until mushrooms are tender. Add tomato paste, cherry tomatoes and 1 cup cold water. Increase heat to high. Bring to the boil. Return chicken to pan. Reduce heat to medium-low. Cook, covered, for 20 minutes or until chicken is cooked through and sauce has slightly thickened. Season with pepper.

3 Meanwhile, cook pasta in a large saucepan of boiling salted water, following packet directions, until tender. Drain.

4 Divide pasta and goulash between serving bowls. Top with sour cream. Serve sprinkled with chives.

NUTRITION: (per serve) 2652kJ; 20.9g fat; 6g sat fat; 46.9g protein; 60.3g carbs; 7.4g fibre; 162mg chol; 245mg sodium.

Lower GI, lower sodium, low saturated fat

CHICKEN SCHNITZEL & AVOCADO SALAD

SERVES 4   **PREP** 10 minutes   **COOK** 12 minutes

1 bunch asparagus, trimmed, cut into thirds
Vegetable oil, for shallow frying (see note)
500g crumbed chicken schnitzel
120g baby rocket
1 large avocado, chopped
¼ cup shaved parmesan
⅓ cup ranch dressing

1 Place asparagus in a heatproof bowl. Cover with boiling water. Stand for 3 minutes or until bright green and tender. Rinse under cold water. Drain.

2 Meanwhile, pour enough oil into a large frying pan to come 5mm up side of pan. Heat over medium-high heat. Cook chicken, in batches, for 3 minutes each side or until cooked through. Transfer to a plate lined with paper towel to drain. Slice.

3 Place rocket in a large bowl. Add asparagus, avocado, parmesan, schnitzel and dressing. Toss to combine. Season and serve.

NUTRITION: (per serve) 2977kJ; 58.2g fat; 12g sat fat; 17.6g protein; 29.7g carbs; 3.3g fibre; 70mg chol; 990mg sodium.

COOK'S NOTE You can bake the schnitzel at 180°C/160°C fan-forced for 15 to 20 minutes if preferred.

CHICKEN & VEGETABLE LAKSA

SERVES 4

PREP 20 minutes

COOK 16 minutes

250g packet dried vermicelli noodles

1 tablespoon vegetable oil

185g jar Malaysian laksa paste

2 cups salt-reduced chicken stock

2 x 270ml cans light coconut milk

2 tablespoons fish sauce

500g chicken breast fillets, thinly sliced

300g broccoli, cut into small florets

150g green beans, trimmed, cut into thirds

125g cherry tomatoes, halved

½ cup fresh mint leaves

2 cups bean sprouts, trimmed

½ cup fried shallots (see note)

Lime wedges, to serve

1 Place noodles in a large, heatproof bowl. Cover with boiling water. Stand for 5 minutes or until noodles soften. Drain.

2 Meanwhile, heat oil in a wok over medium-high heat. Add laksa paste. Cook, stirring, for 2 to 3 minutes or until fragrant. Add stock, coconut milk and fish sauce. Bring to the boil. Add chicken. Reduce heat to medium-low, simmer for 5 minutes. Add broccoli and beans. Simmer for 2 minutes. Add tomato. Simmer for 1 minute or until broccoli is bright green and tender.

3 Divide noodles between bowls. Ladle laksa over noodles. Top with mint, bean sprouts and shallots. Serve with lime wedges.

NUTRITION: (per serve) 2873kJ; 22.9g fat; 8.9g sat fat; 44g protein; 71.5g carbs; 12.2g fibre; 84mg chol; 2172mg sodium.

COOK'S NOTE Fried shallots can be found in the Asian food aisle of major supermarkets.

High fibre

CHICKEN & AVOCADO PASTA SALAD

SERVES 4
PREP 10 minutes
COOK 10 minutes

3 cups dried fusilli pasta
3 cups shredded cooked chicken
½ x 285g jar piquillo peppers, drained, thinly sliced
4 green onions, thinly sliced
2 avocados, sliced
50g baby spinach, roughly shredded
½ cup whole-egg mayonnaise
¼ cup lemon juice
2 tablespoons chopped fresh thyme

1 Cook pasta in a large saucepan of boiling salted water, following packet directions, until tender. Drain. Rinse under cold water. Drain well. Set aside to cool.

2 Place chicken, peppers, onion, avocado, spinach and pasta in a large bowl.

3 Combine mayonnaise, lemon juice and thyme in a small jug. Season with salt and pepper. Drizzle salad with dressing. Toss gently to combine. Serve.

NUTRITION: (per serve) 4181kJ; 57g fat; 10.3g sat fat; 40.3g protein; 77.6g carbs; 6.3g fibre; 131mg chol; 276mg sodium.

COOK'S NOTE Add some crispy bacon to the salad for an extra flavour boost and crunch.

Lower sodium

PEKING CHICKEN CREPES WITH SNOW PEA SALAD

SERVES 4
PREP 30 minutes
COOK 8 minutes

150g snow peas, trimmed
4 green onions
50g snow pea sprouts, trimmed
2 Lebanese cucumbers, halved lengthways, sliced
3 cups chopped cooked chicken
⅔ cup hoisin sauce
400g packet frozen French-style crepes
8 garlic chives

1 Finely shred snow peas and thinly slice onions. Place in a bowl. Add sprouts and cucumber. Toss to combine. Place chicken and hoisin sauce in separate bowls.

2 Heat crepes following packet directions. Place 1 crepe on a plate. Top with one-eighth of the snow pea mixture, chicken and hoisin sauce. Roll up. Secure with a chive. Repeat with remaining crepes, snow pea mixture and hoisin sauce. Serve.

NUTRITION: (per serve) 2255kJ; 17.7g fat; 5g sat fat; 34.7g protein; 57.3g carbs; 7.6g fibre; 107mg chol; 1119mg sodium.

High fibre

CHICKEN NOODLE FRITTERS

SERVES 4   **PREP** 15 minutes   **COOK** 8 minutes

75g packet chicken-flavoured instant noodles
   (see note)
100g green beans, trimmed, thinly sliced
¾ cup self-raising flour
1 egg, separated
¾ cup chopped barbecued chicken
2 tablespoons peanut oil
¼ cup kecap manis

1 Place noodles and beans in a heatproof bowl. Cover with boiling water. Stand for 5 minutes. Drain. Using scissors, roughly chop noodles.

2 Place flour in a bowl. Make a well. Add egg yolk and ½ cup cold water. Whisk until smooth. Add noodle mixture, all 3 seasoning sachets from noodle packet and chicken. Stir to combine. Whisk egg white in a bowl until stiff peaks form. Fold into batter.

3 Heat half the oil in a large frying pan over medium-high heat. Drop ⅓ cup mixture into pan, pressing gently with a spatula to flatten slightly. Repeat 3 more times to form 4 fritters. Cook for 2 minutes each side or until golden and cooked through. Transfer fritters to a plate lined with paper towel. Cover loosely with foil to keep warm. Repeat with remaining batter to make 8 fritters, adding more oil when necessary. Serve fritters drizzled with kecap manis.

NUTRITION: (per serve) 1499kJ; 16.3g fat; 4.4g sat fat; 13.8g protein; 38.3g carbs; 3.1g fibre; 73mg chol; 1089mg sodium.

COOK'S NOTE We used a packet of noodles with 3 seasoning sachets.

Low saturated fat

CHICKEN PARCELS WITH TARRAGON BUTTER

SERVES 4   **PREP** 10 minutes   **COOK** 20 minutes

You'll need four x 22cm pieces of baking paper
2 carrots, thinly sliced diagonally
4 small (about 150g each) chicken breast fillets
60g butter, chopped
⅓ cup dry white wine
4 small fresh tarragon sprigs
Steamed green beans, baby rocket and steamed chat
   potatoes, halved, to serve

1 Preheat oven to 200°C/180°C fan-forced. Place 1 piece baking paper on a flat surface. Place ¼ of the carrot in centre. Top with 1 chicken breast fillet and ¼ of the butter, wine and tarragon. Season with salt and pepper. Bring 2 sides of the paper up to the centre and fold to seal. Roll up the ends to enclose. Place on a baking tray. Repeat with remaining baking paper, carrot, chicken, butter, wine and tarragon.

2 Bake for 20 minutes or until chicken is cooked through. Carefully open parcels, allowing steam to escape. Toss beans through rocket. Serve chicken with potatoes and rocket mixture.

NUTRITION: (per serve) 1805kJ; 14.8g fat; 9g sat fat; 39.3g protein; 27.2g carbs; 9.1g fibre; 136mg chol; 280mg sodium.

High fibre, gluten free, lower sodium

SEAFOOD

DIABETES-FRIENDLY STEAMED GINGER FISH WITH GAI LAN

SERVES 4
PREP 20 minutes
COOK 15 minutes

You'll need four 30cm x 40cm sheets baking paper
1 tablespoon salt-reduced soy sauce
1 garlic clove, crushed
1 tablespoon rice wine vinegar
2 teaspoons mirin (Japanese rice wine)
4 x 120g firm white fish fillets
5cm piece fresh ginger, peeled, cut into matchsticks
2 tablespoons chopped coriander stems (2cm lengths)
2 bunches gai lan (Chinese broccoli), stems and leaves separated, chopped
½ teaspoon sesame oil
3 cups cooked low-GI brown rice
Sliced long red chilli, lime wedges and fresh coriander leaves, to serve

1 Combine soy, garlic, vinegar, mirin and 2 teaspoons cold water in a bowl. Place 1 sheet baking paper on a flat surface. Place 1 fish fillet in centre of paper. Top with ¼ of the ginger and coriander stems. Drizzle with ¼ of the soy mixture. Fold up baking paper to enclose filling. Secure with kitchen string. Repeat with remaining baking paper, fish, ginger, coriander stems and soy mixture.

2 Place a large steamer over a wok or large saucepan of simmering water. Place parcels, seam-side up, in steamer. Cook, covered, for 6 to 8 minutes or until fish is cooked through. Remove steamer from wok. Carefully remove fish from steamer.

3 Place broccoli stems in steamer. Return to wok. Cook, covered, for 3 to 4 minutes or until just tender. Add leaves. Cook, covered, for 1 to 2 minutes or until wilted.

4 Remove and discard string from parcels. Divide broccoli between serving plates. Top with fish and drizzle with sauce from parcel and sesame oil. Serve with rice. Sprinkle with chilli and coriander leaves and serve with lime wedges.

NUTRITION: (per serve) 1476kJ; 4.3g fat; 1.1g sat fat; 33g protein; 40g carbs; 8.2g fibre; 73mg chol; 325mg sodium.

COOK'S NOTES If you have a smaller steamer, cook the fish in 2 batches. You could also use other Asian vegetables such as bok choy.

Healthy, lower GI, diabetes friendly

PAN-FRIED FISH WITH CREAMY MUSTARD SAUCE

SERVES 4   **PREP** 10 minutes   **COOK** 15 minutes

30g butter
4 (150g each) firm white fish fillets
1 tablespoon plain flour
⅓ cup dry white wine
¾ cup fish stock
½ cup thickened cream
1 tablespoon wholegrain mustard
1 tablespoon chopped fresh dill
Steamed chat potatoes, green beans and lemon
    wedges, to serve

1 Melt half the butter in a large non-stick frying pan over medium-high heat. Season fish with salt and pepper. Cook fish for 3 to 4 minutes each side or until just cooked through. Transfer to a plate. Cover with foil.

2 Wipe pan clean. Melt remaining butter in pan. Add flour. Cook, stirring, for 1 minute. Remove from heat. Slowly whisk in wine until smooth. Whisk in stock. Simmer for 1 minute or until thick. Add cream. Simmer for 2 minutes or until thickened. Stir in mustard and dill. Season with salt and pepper.

3 Drizzle fish with sauce and serve with potatoes, beans and lemon wedges.

NUTRITION: (per serve) 1957kJ; 21.7g fat; 12.6g sat fat; 36.5g protein; 25.1g carbs; 5.4g fibre; 141mg chol; 575mg sodium.

Lower sodium

THAI GARLIC PRAWNS

SERVES 4   **PREP** 30 minutes   **COOK** 6 minutes

6 garlic cloves, roughly chopped
2cm piece fresh ginger, peeled, roughly chopped
2 eschalots, peeled, roughly chopped
1 lemongrass stalk (white part only), roughly chopped
1 long red chilli, roughly chopped
½ cup rice bran oil
1kg medium green king prawns, peeled, deveined,
    tails intact
1 tablespoon lime juice
2 teaspoons grated palm sugar
Lime wedges and fresh coriander leaves, to serve

1 Place garlic, ginger, eschalot, lemongrass and chilli in a small food processor. Process until finely chopped.

2 Heat oil in a large, deep frying pan over medium-high heat. Add garlic mixture. Cook, stirring, for 2 minutes or until fragrant. Add prawns. Cook, tossing occasionally, for 3 to 4 minutes or until prawns are pink and cooked through. Remove from heat. Add lime juice and sugar. Toss to combine.

3 Serve prawns in oil mixture with lime wedges and sprinkled with coriander leaves.

NUTRITION: (per serve) 1588kJ; 27.2g fat; 6.1g sat fat; 28.9g protein; 4.3g carbs; 1.5g fibre; 205mg chol; 487mg sodium.

SWEET CHILLI FISH SKEWERS WITH PICKLED CABBAGE SALAD

SERVES 4

PREP 30 minutes

COOK 6 minutes

You'll need 8 pre-soaked bamboo skewers or metal skewers for this recipe

½ cup rice wine vinegar

2 tablespoons caster sugar

250g packet coleslaw mix

1 carrot, grated

4 radishes, trimmed, thinly sliced

5 green onions

½ cup sweet chilli sauce

¼ cup lime juice

3cm piece fresh ginger, finely grated

3 garlic cloves, crushed

700g white fish fillets, cut into 3cm pieces

1 tablespoon rice bran oil

1 tablespoon sesame seeds, toasted

Steamed white long-grain rice, to serve

1 Place vinegar and sugar in a large bowl. Stir until sugar dissolves. Add coleslaw mix, carrot and radish. Toss to combine. Set aside, stirring occasionally, for 30 minutes.

2 Meanwhile, cut white and light green section of onion into 3cm lengths. Thinly slice dark green section. Set aside.

3 Place sweet chilli sauce, lime juice, ginger and garlic in a large bowl. Stir to combine. Add fish. Toss to coat. Thread fish and onion lengths, alternately, onto skewers, reserving marinade.

4 Drizzle oil on a barbecue chargrill. Heat on medium-high heat. Cook skewers, basting with marinade halfway through, for 2 to 3 minutes each side or until cooked through. Toss sesame seeds through coleslaw mixture. Serve salad with fish skewers, steamed rice and sliced green onion.

NUTRITION: (per serve) 2438kJ; 8g fat; 2.2g sat fat; 42.8g protein; 80.1g carbs; 5.2g fibre; 105mg chol; 500mg sodium.

Lower sodium, heart friendly, low saturated fat

Add snow peas. Toss to combine. Serve fish with rice and sprinkle with coriander leaves.

NUTRITION: (per serve)1563kj; fat 11.3g; sat fat 7g; protein 35.2g; carbs 31.1g; fibre 3.8g; chol 79mg; sodium 699 mg.

Low fat

SPICED COCONUT CALAMARI WITH ZESTY GREEN SALAD

SERVES 4   **PREP** 20 minutes   **COOK** 10 minutes
1 teaspoon sichuan peppercorns
2 teaspoons salt
¾ cup desiccated coconut
¼ cup cornflour
Peanut oil, for shallow-frying
600g cleaned calamari hoods, cut into 5mm-wide rings (see note)
Lime wedges, to serve
Zesty green salad
2 cups beansprouts
100g snow peas, shredded
1 long red chilli, seeded, thinly sliced
3 green onions, thinly sliced diagonally
1 cup mint leaves, torn
¾ cup fresh coriander leaves
2 tablespoons lime juice

1 Place sichuan peppercorns in a mortar and pestle. Pound until finely crushed. Add salt. Pound until well combined. Place mixture in a large bowl. Stir in coconut and cornflour.

2 Pour peanut oil into a large, deep frying pan to reach a depth of 5cm. Heat over high heat. Toss calamari in coconut mixture to coat. Cook calamari, in 3 batches, for 2 to 3 minutes or until just cooked through. Transfer to a tray lined with paper towel.

3 Make Zesty green salad Combine all ingredients in a large bowl. Toss well. Serve salad topped with calamari and lime wedges.

NUTRITION: (per serve) 1520kJ; 20.5g fat; 10.4g sat fat; 29.4g protein; 11.8g carbs; 6.3g fibre; 298mg chol; 1651mg sodium.

High fibre

GREEN CURRY FISH PARCELS WITH COCONUT RICE

SERVES 4   **PREP** 20 minutes   **COOK** 15 minutes
You'll need 4 x 10cm pieces baking paper and 4 x 25cm pieces foil
1 tablespoon Thai green curry paste
¼ cup coconut cream
4 (150g each) firm white fish fillets
1 eschalot, thinly sliced
1 long red chilli, thinly sliced diagonally
1 small lime, cut into 8 slices
2 x 250g packets coconut, chilli and lemongrass microwaveable rice
100g snow peas, trimmed, thinly sliced
Fresh coriander leaves, to serve

1 Preheat oven to 200°C/180°C fan-forced. Combine curry paste and coconut cream in a bowl.

2 Place 1 piece baking paper in the centre of 1 piece foil. Top with 1 fish fillet, ¼ curry mixture, ¼ eschalot, ¼ chilli and 2 lime slices. Bring 2 sides of foil up to the centre. Fold to seal. Roll up ends to enclose filling. Place on a baking tray. Repeat with remaining fish. Bake for 15 minutes or until cooked through.

3 Meanwhile, cook coconut, chilli and lemongrass rice following packet directions. Place in a heatproof bowl.

TUNA & NOODLE FRITTERS

SERVES 4 (makes 12 fritters)
PREP 15 minutes
COOK 25 minutes

½ x 440g packet shelf-fresh thin egg noodles
185g can tuna in oil, drained, flaked
½ cup frozen peas
1 medium carrot, grated
2 eggs, lightly beaten
⅓ cup plain flour
2 tablespoons rice bran oil
8 small iceberg lettuce leaves, torn
150g cherry tomatoes, quartered
1 Lebanese cucumber, cut into ribbons
Sweet chilli sauce, to serve

1 Place noodles in a heatproof bowl. Cover with boiling water. Stand for 1 minute. Separate noodles with a fork. Drain. Using scissors, roughly chop noodles. Place noodles, tuna, peas, carrot, egg and flour in a bowl. Season with salt and pepper. Mix until well combined.

2 Heat oil in large non-stick frying pan over medium heat. Spoon ¼ cup mixture into pan. Gently flatten top. Repeat to make 3 more fritters. Cook fritters for 3 to 4 minutes on each side or until golden and cooked through. Transfer to a plate lined with paper towel. Repeat with remaining mixture to make a total of 12 fritters.

3 Arrange lettuce on serving plates. Top each with 3 fritters, tomato and cucumber. Drizzle with sweet chilli sauce. Serve.

NUTRITION: (per serve) 1813kJ; 15.5g fat; 3.4g sat fat; 19.8g protein; 50.4g carbs; 5.1g fibre; 114mg chol; 451mg sodium.

COOK'S NOTE Use any leftover fritters for lunch the next day.

High fibre, low kilojoule, low saturated fat

SUPER-EASY FISH CAKES WITH AIOLI

SERVES 4
PREP 15 minutes
COOK 12 minutes

500g boneless white fish fillets, roughly chopped
2¼ cups fresh breadcrumbs
3 green onions, trimmed, sliced
1 tablespoon chopped fresh dill
1 egg
White pepper, to season
2 tablespoons light olive oil
Aioli, baby rocket and oven-baked potato chips, to serve

1 Process fish, breadcrumbs, onion, dill and egg until almost smooth. Season with salt and white pepper. Using ¼ cup of mixture at a time, shape mixture into 8 patties. Place on a tray lined with baking paper. Cover. Refrigerate.

2 Heat half the oil in a large non-stick frying pan over medium-high heat. Add half the patties to pan. Cook for 3 minutes each side or until golden and cooked through. Transfer to a plate. Repeat with remaining oil and patties.

3 Serve patties immediately with aioli, rocket and chips.

NUTRITION: (per serve) 2630kJ; 35.3g fat; 5.3g sat fat; 35.3g protein; 3.8g carbs; 3.8g fibre; 143mg chol; 603mg sodium.

4 Add fish, coriander, mint, beansprouts, onion and cabbage to noodles. Drizzle with dressing. Gently toss to combine. Serve.

NUTRITION: (per serve) 2059kj; fat 19.8g; sat fat 3.3g; protein 46.1g; carbs 30.1g; fibre 3.9g; chol107mg; sodium 672 mg.

low kilojoule, low saturated fat

SALT & PEPPER SALMON WITH PAPAYA SALSA

SERVES 4
PREP 20 minutes
COOK 8 minutes
1 tablespoon sea salt
1 tablespoon cracked black pepper
1 tablespoon rice bran oil
4 x 100g salmon fillets, skin on
Steamed jasmine rice, lime wedges and fresh
    coriander leaves, to serve
Papaya salsa
½ medium (400g) papaya, finely diced
1 Lebanese cucumber, halved, seeded, thinly sliced
2 kaffir lime leaves, shredded
½ long green chilli, seeded, finely chopped
2 tablespoons lime juice
1 tablespoon fish sauce
2 tablespoons fresh coriander leaves, finely chopped

1 Make Papaya salsa Combine papaya, cucumber, lime leaves, chilli, lime juice, fish sauce and coriander in a small bowl. Set aside.

2 Combine salt and pepper in a small bowl. Sprinkle over both sides of salmon, pressing to stick. Heat oil in a large frying pan over medium heat. Cook salmon, skin-side down, for 3 to 4 minutes (see note). Turn. Cook for 2 to 3 minutes or until golden and cooked to your liking. Serve with papaya salsa, rice, lime wedges and coriander.

NUTRITION: (per serve) 1785kJ; 15.4g fat; 3.4g sat fat; 33.3g protein; 35.4g carbs; 4.1g fibre; 78mg chol; 1715mg sodium.

COOK'S NOTE It's best to cook salmon in 2 batches to ensure skin becomes crisp and salmon doesn't stew.

Low saturated fat

WARM FISH & NOODLE SALAD

SERVES 4
PREP 15 minutes
COOK 12 minutes (plus standing time)
1 tablespoon olive oil
750g firm white fish fillets
350g fresh chow mein noodles
½ cup chopped fresh coriander leaves
½ cup roughly chopped fresh mint leaves
1 cup beansprouts, trimmed
6 green onions, thinly sliced
3 cups shredded Chinese cabbage (wombok)
Chilli lime dressing
⅓ cup lime juice
2 tablespoons olive oil
1 tablespoon soy sauce
1 teaspoon brown sugar
1 red birdseye chilli, seeded, finely chopped

1 Make Chilli lime dressing Place ingredients in a screw-top jar. Secure lid. Shake to combine.

2 Heat oil in a frying pan over medium-high heat. Cook fish for 3 minutes each side or until cooked through. Transfer to a plate. Using a fork, flake fish. Cover.

3 Meanwhile, place noodles in a large bowl. Cover with boiling water for 2 to 3 minutes or until tender. Using a fork, separate noodles. Drain.

OVEN-BAKED GARLIC & CHILLI PRAWN RISOTTO

SERVES 4

PREP 10 minutes

COOK 30 minutes

3 garlic cloves

2 tablespoons olive oil

1 medium red onion, thinly sliced

1½ cups arborio rice

1 litre salt-reduced chicken or fish stock

1 long red chilli, thinly sliced (see note)

¼ cup small fresh basil leaves

12 medium green king prawns, peeled, deveined, tails intact

150g cherry tomatoes, halved

1 Preheat oven to 180°C/160°C fan-forced. Crush 1 garlic clove. Thinly slice remaining garlic. Heat half the oil in a large, flameproof casserole dish over medium heat. Add the onion. Cook, stirring, for 5 minutes or until softened. Add the crushed garlic. Cook, stirring, for 1 minute.

2 Add rice. Stir to coat. Add stock and chilli. Stir to combine. Bring to the boil. Cover with foil. Transfer to oven. Bake for 10 minutes or until half the liquid has been absorbed.

3 Meanwhile, heat the remaining oil in a medium frying pan over medium heat. Add basil and sliced garlic. Cook for 1 to 2 minutes or until golden and crisp. Use a slotted spoon to transfer garlic and basil to a plate lined with paper towel. Discard oil.

4 Remove foil from the risotto. Top with prawns and tomatoes, cut side-up. Bake for 10 minutes or until liquid has almost absorbed and the prawns are cooked through. Remove from oven. Season with pepper. Serve topped with garlic and basil.

NUTRITION: (per serve) 1744kJ; 6.6g fat; 1g sat fat; 21.2g protein; 66.1g carbs; 1.9g fibre; 90mg chol; 836mg sodium.

COOK'S NOTE To reduce the heat, remove the seeds from the chilli.

Low saturated fat

TUNA, BROAD BEAN & RISONI SALAD

SERVES 4
PREP 15 minutes (plus standing time)
COOK 8 minutes
2 cups frozen broad beans
1½ cups dried risoni
425g can tuna chunks in springwater
250g fresh ricotta, crumbled
2 teaspoons finely grated lemon rind
¼ cup lemon juice
1 tablespoon extra virgin olive oil
2 tablespoons chopped fresh mint leaves
2 tablespoons fresh mint leaves, to serve

1 Place broad beans in a heatproof bowl. Cover with boiling water. Stand for 5 minutes. Peel and discard skins.

2 Cook risoni in a saucepan of boiling salted water until tender, adding broad beans in the last minute of cooking. Drain well. Transfer to a heatproof bowl.

3 Add drained tuna, ricotta, lemon rind, juice, oil and mint to pasta. Season. Toss to combine. Serve sprinkled with mint leaves.

NUTRITION: (per serve) 2248kJ; 14.9g fat; 6g sat fat; 40.5g protein; 54.5g carbs; 9g fibre; 69mg chol; 245mg sodium.

High fibre, lower sodium, low saturated fat

FISH WITH AVOCADO SALSA

SERVES 4
PREP 12 minutes
COOK 8 minutes
1 medium avocado, diced
1 Lebanese cucumber, seeded, diced
1 tablespoon lime juice
1 green chilli, seeded, finely chopped
1 tablespoon olive oil
4 (150g each) firm white fish fillets
¼ cup fresh coriander sprigs
Steamed rice and lime cheeks, to serve

1 Place avocado, cucumber, lime juice and chilli in a bowl. Season with salt and pepper. Stir gently to combine. Cover. Refrigerate.

2 Heat oil in a large non-stick frying pan over high heat. Cook fish for 2 minutes each side or until cooked through. Serve fish with salsa, coriander sprigs, steamed rice and lime cheeks.

NUTRITION: (per serve) 2175kj; fat 15.7g; sat fat 3.2g; protein 35.6g; carbs 54.4g; fibre 2.7g; chol 69mg; sodium 206 mg.

Gluten free, low saturated fat

FISH WITH COCONUT RICE & LIME & CORIANDER GREMOLATA

SERVES 4
PREP 10 minutes
COOK 12 minutes

1½ cups jasmine rice, rinsed
270ml can light coconut milk
⅓ cup chopped fresh coriander leaves
2 teaspoons finely grated lime rind
2 garlic cloves, crushed
1 long red chilli, finely chopped (see notes)
4 (150g each) firm white fish fillets, skin on (see notes)
2 teaspoons peanut oil
1 tablespoon soy sauce
Lime wedges, to serve

1 Place rice in a saucepan. Add coconut milk and 1¼ cups cold water. Stir to combine. Bring to the boil over high heat. Stir. Cover. Reduce heat to low. Simmer for 10 to 12 minutes or until liquid has absorbed. Using a fork, fluff rice to separate grains.

2 Meanwhile, place coriander, lime rind, garlic and chilli in a bowl. Stir until well combined.

3 Drizzle fish with oil. Season with pepper. Heat a large frying pan or barbecue plate on medium-high heat. Cook fish for 3 to 4 minutes each side or until cooked through.

4 Divide rice between plates. Top with fish. Drizzle with soy and sprinkle with gremolata. Serve with lime wedges.

NUTRITION: (per serve) 2119kJ; 10.6g fat; 5.8g sat fat; 38g protein; 62.6g carbs; 1.6g fibre; 84mg chol; 450mg sodium.

COOK'S NOTES For less heat, remove seeds from chilli. You could use blue-eye or barramundi fillets.

Lower sodium, low saturated fat

GRILLED FISH WITH BANANA, MANGO & CHILLI SALSA

SERVES 4
PREP 15 minutes
COOK 10 minutes

1 tablespoon olive oil
4 x 150g firm white fish fillets (see note)
2 medium bananas, finely chopped
1 medium mango, finely chopped
1 long red chilli, seeded, finely chopped
¼ cup finely chopped fresh coriander leaves
1 tablespoon lime juice
Mixed salad leaves and lime wedges, to serve

1 Heat oil in a large frying pan over medium-high heat. Add fish. Cook for 3 to 4 minutes each side or until cooked through.

2 Meanwhile, combine banana, mango, chilli, coriander and lime juice in a medium bowl. Mix well. Serve fish with salsa, mixed salad leaves and lime wedges.

NUTRITION: (per serve) 1068kJ; 6.5g fat; 1g sat fat; 29.8g protein; 17.9g carbs; 2.6g fibre; 47mg chol; 135mg sodium.

COOK'S NOTE We used perch. You could also use ling or blue-eye.

Low fat, low kilojoule, lower sodium

TOMATO, HERB & PINE NUT SALMON

SERVES 8

PREP 20 minutes

COOK 30 minutes

1.5kg salmon fillet (1 whole side of salmon), bones removed

½ cup plain Greek-style yoghurt

2 green onions, finely chopped

2 garlic cloves, crushed

½ cup firmly packed fresh mint leaves, chopped

½ cup firmly packed fresh flat-leaf parsley leaves, chopped

2 tablespoons chopped fresh dill

3 tomatoes, seeded, finely chopped

¼ cup toasted pine nuts

2 tablespoons drained capers, chopped

2 tablespoons lemon juice

1 tablespoon extra virgin olive oil

Lemon wedges, to serve

1 Preheat oven to 180°C/160°C fan-forced. Line a large baking tray with foil, then baking paper. Place salmon, skin-side down, on baking paper. Spread yoghurt over top of salmon.

2 Combine onion, garlic, mint, parsley, dill, tomato, pine nuts, capers, lemon juice and oil in a bowl. Press mixture evenly over yoghurt layer. Season well with salt and pepper.

3 Bake salmon for 25 to 30 minutes or until cooked to your liking. Serve with lemon wedges.

NUTRITION: (per serve) 1479kJ; 20.5g fat; 4.4g sat fat; 37.3g protein; 3.5g carbs; 2g fibre; 95mg chol; 155mg sodium.

Lower sodium

POACHED SALMON & ORANGE SALAD

SERVES 4
PREP 10 minutes
COOK 15 minutes

4 oranges
6 sprigs fresh thyme
½ teaspoon black peppercorns
4 (200g each) salmon fillets, skin on
1 tablespoon extra virgin olive oil
80g baby rocket
1 Lebanese cucumber, halved lengthways, sliced
1 avocado, cut into 2cm pieces

1 Juice 2 oranges (you'll need 1 cup juice). Place orange juice, thyme, peppercorns and 3 cups cold water in a large, deep frying pan over medium heat. Bring to a simmer. Reduce heat to low. Add salmon. Cook, covered, for 10 minutes or until cooked to your liking. Using a spatula, remove salmon from liquid. Flake into large pieces.

2 Finely grate rind from 1 orange. Peel oranges and segment. Squeeze membrane over a bowl to catch juice (you will need 2 tablespoons juice). Discard membrane. Place oil and orange juice in a screw-top jar. Season with salt and pepper. Secure lid. Shake to combine.

3 Combine rocket, orange segments, cucumber and avocado in a bowl. Arrange salmon on salad. Drizzle with dressing. Serve.

NUTRITION: (per serve) 1872kJ; 28.1g fat; 5.8g sat fat; 40.9g protein; 7.2g carbs; 1.7g fibre; 104mg chol; 160mg sodium.

Lower sodium, low saturated fat

SWEET & SOUR FISH

SERVES 4

PREP 20 minutes

COOK 16 minutes

500g firm white fish fillets, cut into 2.5cm pieces

Olive oil cooking spray

1 tablespoon cornflour

1 tablespoon salt-reduced soy sauce

2 tablespoons cider vinegar

200g fresh pineapple, roughly chopped

1 tablespoon pineapple juice

2 tablespoons salt-reduced tomato sauce

½ small red onion, cut into thin wedges

½ red capsicum, cut into 2cm pieces

½ green capsicum, cut into 2cm pieces

1 medium carrot, cut into matchsticks

120g sugar snap peas, trimmed

Steamed brown rice, to serve

1 Season fish lightly with salt and pepper. Toss lightly to coat. Spray lightly with oil.

2 Heat a non-stick frying pan over medium-high heat. Cook fish, in batches, for 1 minute on each side or until golden and cooked through. Wipe pan clean.

3 Blend cornflour with 1 tablespoon cold water in a bowl until smooth. Add soy sauce, vinegar, pineapple, juice and tomato sauce. Stir well.

4 Spray oil in pan over medium-high heat. Add onion, capsicum and carrot. Cook, stirring, for 5 minutes or until vegetables are almost tender. Add pineapple mixture. Stir to combine. Bring to the boil. Reduce heat to low. Add peas. Simmer for 3 minutes. Add fish to sauce mixture. Simmer for 1 minute or until heated through. Serve on steamed brown rice.

NUTRITION: (per serve) 2447kJ; 5.1g fat; 0.9g sat fat; 35.2g protein; 94.1g carbs; 6.9g fibre; 57mg chol; 502mg sodium.

High fibre, lower sodium, low saturated fat

CRISPY FISH TORTILLAS

SERVES 4

PREP 20 minutes

COOK 5 minutes

1 egg

30g packet taco spice mix

¾ cup panko breadcrumbs

500g firm white fish fillets, cut into 4cm pieces

Rice bran oil, for shallow frying

8 small flour tortillas

¼ iceberg lettuce, roughly torn

2 tomatoes, sliced

½ red onion, thinly sliced

1 avocado, sliced

1 cup fresh coriander leaves

Lime wedges and Tabasco sauce (optional), to serve

1 Place egg and 1 tablespoon cold water in a shallow bowl. Lightly whisk to combine. Place spice mix in a shallow bowl. Place breadcrumbs on a plate.

2 Press fish in spice mix to coat. Dip fish in egg mixture, shaking off excess. Toss fish in breadcrumbs to coat. Place on a plate.

3 Pour enough oil into a frying pan to come 1cm up side of pan. Heat over medium-high heat. Cook fish, in 2 batches, for 2 minutes, turning, or until golden and cooked through. Drain on paper towel.

4 Meanwhile, heat a chargrill on high. Chargrill tortillas, in batches, for 1 minute or until lightly charred and warm. Serve fish and tortillas with lettuce, tomato, onion, avocado, coriander, lime wedges and Tabasco sauce (if using).

NUTRITION: (per serve) 2984kJ; 30.9g fat; 8.2g sat fat; 38g protein; 66.8g carbs; 5.9g fibre; 111mg chol; 1567mg sodium.

High fibre

SPRING VEGETABLE & PRAWN RISOTTO WITH LEMON & DILL OIL

SERVES 4

PREP 15 minutes

COOK 30 minutes (plus 5 minutes resting)

2 teaspoons finely grated lemon rind

2 teaspoons fresh dill leaves, finely chopped

⅓ cup extra virgin olive oil

6 cups salt-reduced vegetable stock

1 large brown onion, finely chopped

2 garlic cloves, crushed

1½ cups arborio rice

1 bunch asparagus, trimmed, cut into 3cm lengths

½ cup frozen baby peas

50g baby spinach

100g medium green prawns, peeled, deveined, halved lengthways

¼ cup goat's cheese (see note)

¼ cup pine nuts, toasted

1 Combine lemon rind, dill and 2 tablespoons oil in a bowl. Season with salt and pepper. Set aside to allow flavours to develop.

2 Place stock in a medium saucepan over medium-high heat. Bring to a simmer. Reduce heat to low.

3 Meanwhile, heat remaining oil in a large saucepan over medium heat. Add onion. Cook, stirring, for 5 minutes, or until onion has softened. Add garlic. Cook, stirring, for 1 minute or until fragrant. Add rice. Cook, stirring, for 1 minute to coat in oil mixture. Reduce heat to low. Add ⅓ cup hot stock to rice mixture. Cook, stirring constantly, until stock is absorbed. Repeat with remaining stock, adding ⅓ cup at a time, until all liquid has been absorbed and rice is tender and creamy (about 20 to 25 minutes).

4 Add asparagus, peas, spinach and prawns with the last ⅓ cup hot stock. Season with salt and pepper. Stir gently to combine. Remove pan from heat. Stand, covered, for 5 minutes or until prawns have changed colour and are cooked through.

5 Spoon risotto into serving bowls. Sprinkle with goat's cheese and pine nuts. Serve drizzled with lemon and dill oil.

NUTRITION: (per serve) 2707kJ; 30.9g fat; 5.2g sat fat; 16g protein; 73.4g carbs; 5g fibre; 30mg chol; 1782mg sodium.

COOK'S NOTE We used a soft goat's cheese for this recipe.

High fibre, low saturated fat

TEMPURA FISH WITH CHIPS & SALAD

SERVES 4
PREP 10 minutes
COOK 20 minutes

500g bag frozen beer batter thick and
   chunky potato fries
500g thick boneless white fish fillets (see note)
Vegetable oil, for shallow-frying
150g sachet tempura batter mix
¾ cup iced water
2 tablespoons French salad dressing
Lemon wedges, to serve
Salad
100g baby salad leaves
250g cherry tomatoes, halved
2 Lebanese cucumbers, diced
2 green onions, thinly sliced

1 Make Salad Place baby salad leaves, tomato, cucumber and onion in a bowl. Toss to combine.

2 Preheat oven to 230°C/210°C fan-forced. Line a large baking tray with baking paper. Place fries, in a single layer, on prepared tray. Bake, turning halfway during cooking, for 20 minutes or until golden and crisp.

3 Meanwhile, pat fish dry with paper towel. Cut into 8 equal pieces. Pour vegetable oil into a large non-stick frying pan until 3cm deep. Heat over medium-high heat. Place batter mix in a medium bowl. Slowly add iced water, whisking constantly until smooth. Dip fish into batter to coat, allowing excess batter to drain off. Cook fish, in batches, for 2 to 3 minutes each side or until golden and crisp. Drain on a wire rack over a baking tray.

4 Drizzle salad with salad dressing. Toss to combine. Serve fish with fries, salad and lemon wedges.

COOK'S NOTE We used ling. You could use blue-eye or barramundi instead.

NUTRITION: (per serve) 2314kj; fat 17.8g; sat fat 2.3g; protein 32.6g; carbs 61.9g; fibre 8.8g; chol 66mg; sodium 942 mg.

High fibre

SALMON WITH GREEK RICE SALAD

SERVES 4
PREP 10 minutes
COOK 35 minutes

2 x 270g packets frozen Atlantic salmon provencale
450g packet 2½ minute long grain white rice
200g mini roma tomatoes, halved lengthways
2 Lebanese cucumbers, diced
½ cup fresh flat-leaf parsley leaves, chopped
½ small red onion, thinly sliced
⅔ cup crumbled fetta cheese
2 tablespoons lemon juice
2 tablespoons extra virgin olive oil
Lemon wedges, to serve

1 Cook fish following packet directions.

2 Meanwhile, cook rice following packet directions. Place rice in a large bowl. Using a fork, stir to separate grains. Set aside for 5 minutes to cool. Add tomato, cucumber, parsley, onion and fetta. Drizzle with lemon juice and oil. Season with salt and pepper. Toss to combine.

3 Serve salmon with rice salad and lemon wedges.

NUTRITION: (per serve) 2719kj; fat 35.6g; sat fat 10.6g; protein 38.6g; carbs 45.9g; fibre 3g; chol 101mg; sodium 1096 mg.

OCEAN TROUT & SPRING VEGETABLE SALAD

SERVES 4

PREP 8 minutes

COOK 22 minutes (plus 5 minutes cooling time)

700g chat potatoes

2 tablespoons white vinegar

6 sprigs dill

500g ocean trout fillets, skin on

500g fresh broad beans

2 tablespoons lemon juice

1 tablespoon dijon mustard

¼ cup extra virgin olive oil

1 bunch watercress, washed, cut into small sprigs

3 green onions, thinly sliced

40g snow pea sprouts, roughly chopped

1 Place potatoes and 1 tablespoon cold water in a microwave-safe bowl. Cover. Microwave on HIGH (100%) for 8 minutes or until tender. Drain. Halve.

2 Meanwhile, half fill a medium, deep frying pan with cold water. Add vinegar and half the dill. Bring to a gentle simmer over medium heat. Reduce heat to low. Simmer for 5 minutes or until dill softens. Add trout. Cook, covered, for 4 to 5 minutes or until trout is just cooked through. Using a spatula, remove trout from liquid and transfer to a plate. Set aside for 5 minutes to cool. Remove and discard skin. Flake trout.

3 Remove broad beans from pods. Bring a saucepan of water to the boil over high heat. Cook beans for 3 to 4 minutes or until just tender. Drain. Rinse under cold water. Peel and discard shells.

4 Combine lemon juice and mustard in a bowl. Slowly whisk in oil until thickened. Season with salt and pepper. Remove leaves from remaining dill sprigs. Combine watercress, potato, trout, onion, beans, sprouts and remaining dill in a bowl. Drizzle over dressing. Gently toss to coat. Serve.

NUTRITION: (per serve) 2140kj; fat 26g; sat fat 5.3g; protein 35.3g; carbs 28.2g; fibre 9.8g; chol 72mg; sodium 270 mg.

High in omega-3

BENGALI FISH CURRY

SERVES 6
PREP 15 minutes
COOK 20 minutes

2 tablespoons vegetable oil
1 brown onion, finely chopped
2 garlic cloves, finely chopped
3cm piece fresh ginger, finely grated
10 fresh curry leaves
1 tomato, finely chopped
270ml can coconut milk
1kg firm white fish fillets, cut into 4cm pieces
¼ cup fresh coriander leaves
Spice mix
2 teaspoons yellow mustard seeds
½ teaspoon ground fennel
½ teaspoon hot chilli powder
1 teaspoon ground turmeric
1 teaspoon ground coriander

1 Make Spice mix Combine all ingredients in a bowl.

2 Heat oil in a large saucepan over medium-high heat. Add onion. Cook, stirring, for 5 minutes or until softened. Add garlic, ginger, curry leaves and spice mix. Cook, stirring, for 2 minutes or until mustard seeds start to pop. Add tomato and 1½ cups cold water. Bring to the boil. Reduce heat to low. Simmer for 5 minutes.

3 Add coconut milk. Bring to a simmer. Add fish. Cook for 5 minutes or until fish is just cooked through. Season with salt and pepper. Serve topped with coriander leaves.

NUTRITION: (per serve) 1408kJ; 19.5g fat; 10.2g sat fat; 35.5g protein; 4g carbs; 2.1g fibre; 99mg chol; 250mg sodium.

Lower sodium

PASTA

3 Add olives, ¼ cup basil, gnocchi and reserved cooking liquid to sausage mixture. Toss over medium heat for 1 to 2 minutes. Serve with parmesan and remaining basil.

NUTRITION: 2591kJ; 31.5g fat; 12.9g sat fat; 24.3g protein; 57.4g carbs; 5.9g fibre; 61mg chol; 1881mg sodium.

ZUCCHINI, BACON & FETTA SPAGHETTI

SERVES 4 **PREP** 10 minutes **COOK** 15 minutes

375g dried spaghetti
2 tablespoons extra virgin olive oil
125g shortcut bacon rashers, trimmed, cut into 1cm-thick strips
2 garlic cloves, thinly sliced
4 zucchini, cut into thin ribbons
1 cup fresh flat-leaf parsley leaves
100g fetta, crumbled

1 Cook pasta in a large saucepan of boiling salted water, following packet directions, until tender. Drain, reserving ¼ cup cooking liquid.

2 Heat oil in a large, deep frying pan over medium-high heat. Add bacon. Cook for 3 to 4 minutes or until golden. Add garlic. Cook for 1 minute or until fragrant. Add zucchini. Cook, tossing, for 3 to 4 minutes or until tender.

3 Add pasta and reserved cooking liquid to zucchini mixture in pan. Toss for 2 minutes or until heated through. Add parsley and fetta. Season with salt and pepper. Gently toss to combine. Serve.

NUTRITION: (per serve) 2404kJ; 21.5g fat; 7.2g sat fat; 22.2g protein; 68.3g carbs; 7.8g fibre; 30mg chol; 710mg sodium.

High fibre

GNOCCHI WITH SAUSAGE, TOMATOES & EGGPLANT

SERVES 4 **PREP** 15 minutes **COOK** 15 minutes

6 (450g) thick lamb sausages
1 tablespoon olive oil
1 medium eggplant, cut into 2cm pieces
1 medium brown onion, finely chopped
1 garlic clove, crushed
250g grape tomatoes, halved
500g packet potato gnocchi
½ cup pitted kalamata olives
⅓ cup shredded fresh basil leaves
½ cup shaved parmesan

1 Squeeze meat from sausages and chop into 2cm pieces. Discard skins.

2 Heat oil in a large frying pan over medium-high heat. Add lamb. Cook, stirring, for 2 to 3 minutes or until golden brown. Add eggplant and onion. Cook, stirring, for 3 to 4 minutes or until eggplant is golden. Add garlic and tomatoes. Cook, stirring occasionally, for 5 minutes or until tomatoes soften and start to break down.

2 Meanwhile, cook gnocchi in a large saucepan of boiling salted water, following packet directions, until just tender. Drain, reserving ½ cup of the cooking liquid.

AGNOLOTTI WITH QUICK TOMATO & BASIL SAUCE

SERVES 4 **PREP** 5 minutes **COOK** 10 minutes

625g packet fresh ricotta and spinach agnolotti
⅓ cup olive oil
1 brown onion, finely chopped
250g cherry tomatoes, halved
2 garlic cloves, thinly sliced
½ cup grated parmesan
⅓ cup pitted kalamata olives, thickly sliced
⅓ cup roughly chopped fresh basil leaves
Extra grated parmesan, to serve

1 Cook pasta in a saucepan of boiling salted water, following packet directions, until tender. Drain.

2 Meanwhile, heat oil in a large frying pan over medium-high heat. Add onion. Cook, stirring, for 5 minutes until softened and golden. Add tomatoes and garlic. Cook, stirring, for 2 minutes until tomatoes start to soften.

3 Add pasta, parmesan, olives and basil to pan. Gently toss to combine. Season. Serve sprinkled with extra parmesan.

NUTRITION: (per serve) 2989kJ; 36.6g fat; 13.8g sat fat; 24.6g protein; 70.8g carbs; 7.5g fibre; 28mg chol; 1160mg sodium.

High fibre

HAM, ROCKET & TORTELLINI SALAD

SERVES 4 **PREP** 12 minutes **COOK** 8 minutes

625g packet fresh spinach and ricotta tortellini
200g sliced leg ham, roughly chopped
½ cup Spanish black olives
150g tub roasted peppers, drained, roughly chopped
50g baby rocket
2 green onions, thinly sliced
2 tablespoons extra virgin olive oil

1 Cook tortellini in a large saucepan of boiling salted water for 6 minutes or until tender. Drain. Refresh under cold water. Drain. Place in a large bowl.

2 Add ham, olives, peppers, rocket and onion to tortellini. Season with salt and pepper. Drizzle with oil. Toss to combine. Serve.

NUTRITION: (per serve) 2483kj; fat 20.8g; sat fat 6.2g; protein 26.7g; carbs 73g; fibre 6.2g; chol 102mg; sodium 1744 mg.

High fibre

GARLIC PRAWN & SQUID PASTA WITH CRUNCHY CRUMBS

SERVES 4
PREP 20 minutes
COOK 15 minutes

375g dried castellane pasta (see notes)
400g garlic-marinated peeled green prawns, halved
   lengthways (see notes)
2 cleaned squid hoods, halved lengthways,
   thinly sliced
⅓ cup extra virgin olive oil
½ cup fresh breadcrumbs
400g grape tomatoes
1 long red chilli, seeded, thinly sliced
45g can anchovies in oil, drained, finely chopped
¼ cup finely chopped fresh basil leaves
¼ cup chopped fresh flat-leaf parsley leaves

1 Cook pasta in a large saucepan of boiling salted water, following packet directions, until tender. Drain, reserving ½ cup cooking liquid.

2 Meanwhile, place prawns and squid in a medium bowl. Add 1 tablespoon of the oil. Toss to coat. Heat a greased barbecue hotplate or chargrill on medium-high heat. Cook prawns and squid for 2 minutes or until just cooked through. Transfer to a clean bowl. Cover to keep warm.

3 Heat ½ the remaining oil in a large frying pan over medium-high heat. Add breadcrumbs. Cook, stirring, for 3 to 4 minutes or until golden. Transfer to a bowl.

4 Cut ½ the tomatoes in half. Add remaining oil to pan. Add chilli and anchovies. Cook for 1 minute or until softened. Add tomatoes. Cook for 4 to 5 minutes or until slightly softened. Add reserved cooking liquid. Cook for 1 to 2 minutes or until slightly thickened. Add prawns, squid and pasta. Reduce heat to low. Toss for 1 to 2 minutes or until heated through. Remove from heat.

5 Add basil and parsley to pasta. Toss to combine. Divide pasta between bowls. Serve sprinkled with breadcrumbs.

NUTRITION: (per serve) 2786kJ; 22.3g fat; 3.4g sat fat; 40.6g protein; 71.7g carbs; 5.8g fibre; 250mg chol; 980mg sodium.

COOK'S NOTES
• Any short, thick-style pasta will work well – try rigatoni or penne.
• Supermarkets sell marinated garlic prawns, or you can add 3 crushed garlic cloves to pan with tomatoes.
• For a spicier sauce, keep the seeds in the chilli.

High fibre, lower GI, low saturated fat

PENNE WITH BROCCOLI, FETTA & ROCKET ALMOND PESTO

SERVES 4
PREP 15 minutes
COOK 15 minutes

375g dried penne pasta
1 large head broccoli, cut into small florets
150g fetta, crumbled
Rocket and almond pesto
1 cup firmly packed rocket leaves
1 garlic clove, quartered
1 tablespoon grated parmesan
1 tablespoon slivered almonds, toasted
2 tablespoons olive oil
1 tablespoon lemon juice

1 Cook pasta in a large saucepan of boiling salted water, following packet directions, until tender, adding broccoli for the last 3 minutes of cooking. Drain. Return pasta and broccoli to pan.

2 Meanwhile make Rocket and almond pesto
Place rocket, garlic, parmesan and almonds in a food processor. Process until finely chopped. With motor operating, gradually add combined oil and lemon juice until pesto is almost smooth. Season with salt.

3 Add pesto and half the fetta to pan. Toss gently to combine. Season with pepper. Serve pasta sprinkled with remaining fetta.

NUTRITION: (per serve) 2328kJ; 21.7g fat; 7.7g sat fat; 21.6g protein; 65.1g carbs; 6g fibre; 27mg chol; 490mg sodium.

Lower GI, high fibre, low saturated fat

SPINACH & RICOTTA FRYING PAN LASAGNE

SERVES 4   **PREP** 15 minutes   **COOK** 25 minutes
You'll need a frying pan with an ovenproof handle
1 tablespoon olive oil
1 medium brown onion, finely chopped
2 garlic cloves, crushed
400g can diced tomatoes with oregano and basil
250g baby spinach
250g fresh ricotta, crumbled
100g leg ham, thickly sliced
4 sheets fresh lasagne, cut into thirds
50g mozzarella, thinly sliced
50g tasty cheese, thinly sliced
Mixed salad leaves, to serve

1 Heat half the oil in an 18cm (base), heavy-based, ovenproof non-stick frying pan over medium-high heat. Add onion and garlic. Cook, stirring, for 3 minutes or until onion has softened. Add tomato. Season with salt and pepper. Bring to the boil. Reduce heat to low. Simmer for 5 minutes or until thickened. Transfer to a bowl. Wipe pan clean.

2 Meanwhile, place spinach in a heatproof bowl. Cover with boiling water. Stand for 5 minutes or until wilted. Drain. Squeeze out any excess liquid. Roughly chop. Transfer to a bowl. Add ricotta. Season with salt and pepper. Stir to combine.

3 Drizzle remaining oil over base of pan. Arrange 3 pieces of lasagne over base of pan. Top with one-third ricotta mixture, one-third ham and one-quarter tomato mixture. Repeat layers twice. Top with remaining 3 pieces of lasagne. Spoon over remaining tomato mixture. Top with cheeses. Preheat grill on high.

4 Return pan to medium-low heat. Cook, covered, for 8 to 10 minutes or until lasagne sheets are tender. Grill, uncovered, for 4 minutes or until cheese is melted and golden. Serve with mixed salad leaves.

NUTRITION: (per serve)1713kj; fat 20.6g; sat fat 10.1g; protein 24.3g; carbs 30.5g; fibre 6.2g; chol 45mg; sodium 1100 mg.

High fibre

TUNA, TOMATO & EGGPLANT LINGUINE

SERVES 4   **PREP** 15 minutes   **COOK** 20 minutes
1 large eggplant, thinly sliced
1 lemon
375g dried linguine pasta
2 tablespoons olive oil
6 large (600g) ripe roma tomatoes, chopped
425g can tuna in oil, drained
½ cup roughly chopped fresh flat-leaf parsley leaves

1 Heat a greased barbecue plate or chargrill on medium-high heat. Cook eggplant, turning, for 5 minutes or until charred and tender. When cool enough to handle, cut into thin strips. Finely grate rind from lemon. Segment lemon, discarding membrane. Cook pasta in a large saucepan of boiling salted water, following packet directions, until tender. Drain.

3 Meanwhile, heat oil in a large, deep frying pan over medium-high heat. Add tomato and tuna. Cook for 5 minutes or until tomatoes start to soften. Add eggplant and pasta. Toss gently for 2 minutes or until combined and heated through. Add lemon rind, lemon segments and parsley. Serve pasta immediately.

NUTRITION: (per serve) 2593kj; fat 20.8g; sat fat 3.1g; protein 31.7g; carbs 70.5g; fibre 8.7g; chol 30mg; sodium 380 mg.

Low saturated fat, high fibre

CREAMY MUSHROOM & CHICKEN PASTA

SERVES 4　　**PREP** 20 minutes　　**COOK** 15 minutes

375g dried fettuccine pasta
1½ tablespoons olive oil
2 (500g total) chicken breast fillets
1 small brown onion, finely chopped
150g Swiss brown mushrooms, sliced
150g cup mushrooms, sliced
3 garlic cloves, crushed
1 tablespoon fresh lemon thyme leaves
1 teaspoon finely grated lemon rind
2 teaspoons plain flour
⅓ cup dry white wine
300ml light thickened cream for cooking
Grated parmesan and extra lemon thyme sprigs,
　　to serve

1 Cook pasta in a large saucepan of boiling salted water, following packet directions, until just tender.

2 Meanwhile, heat 2 teaspoons oil in a large, deep frying pan over medium-high heat. Add chicken. Cook for 5 minutes each side or until browned and cooked through. Transfer to a plate. Cover. Rest for 5 minutes.

3 Meanwhile, heat remaining oil in pan over medium-high heat. Add onion. Cook, stirring, for 2 minutes or until softened. Add mushrooms. Cook for 3 to 4 minutes or until just tender. Add garlic, thyme and lemon rind. Cook for 30 seconds or until fragrant. Add flour. Cook, stirring, for 1 minute or until coated. Add wine. Bring to the boil, stirring. Reduce heat to low. Add cream. Stir to combine. Simmer for 2 to 3 minutes or until heated through.

4 Thinly slice chicken. Drain pasta. Add pasta and chicken to mushroom mixture. Season with salt and pepper. Cook, stirring, for 1 to 2 minutes or until heated through. Spoon into bowls. Top with grated parmesan and extra thyme. Serve.

NUTRITION: (per serve) 3048kJ; 25.6g fat; 12.2g sat fat; 45.9g protein; 71.5g carbs; 5.9g fibre; 125mg chol; 265mg sodium.

High fibre, lower sodium

ZUCCHINI & RICOTTA PASTA

SERVES 4　　**PREP** 15 minutes　　**COOK** 15 minutes

375g dried rigatoni pasta
2 medium zucchini, trimmed
2 tablespoons olive oil
2 garlic cloves, crushed
2 teaspoons fresh thyme leaves
150g baby spinach
¼ cup finely grated parmesan
200g fresh ricotta, crumbled
¼ cup pine nuts
½ cup fresh breadcrumbs

1 Cook pasta in a large saucepan of boiling salted water, following packet directions, until tender. Drain, reserving ¼ cup liquid. Place pasta in a large heatproof bowl.

2 Meanwhile, using a vegetable peeler, cut zucchini lengthways into thin ribbons. Heat half the oil in a frying pan over medium-high heat. Add zucchini, garlic and thyme. Cook for 3 to 4 minutes or until zucchini is just tender. Add spinach. Cook until just wilted. Add to pasta with parmesan, ricotta and reserved liquid. Stir.

3 Heat remaining oil in pan over medium-high heat. Add pine nuts. Cook, stirring, for 1 minute or until light golden. Add breadcrumbs. Cook, stirring, for 1 to 2 minutes or until golden. Serve pasta sprinkled with pine nut crumble.

NUTRITION: (per serve) 2605kj; fat 25.6g; sat fat 6.6g; protein 20.9g; carbs 73.3g; fibre 7.2g; chol 36mg; sodium 400 mg.

ALFREDO SAUCE

SERVES 4   **PREP** 15 minutes   **COOK** 15 minutes

375g dried fettuccine
25g butter
4 garlic cloves, crushed
300ml thickened cream
2 tablespoons chopped flat-leaf parsley leaves
⅓ cup finely grated parmesan cheese

1 Cook pasta in a large saucepan of boiling salted water, following packet directions, until tender. Drain, reserving ¼ cup liquid.

2 Melt butter in a large non-stick frying pan over medium heat. Add garlic. Cook, stirring, for 1 minute or until fragrant.

3 Stir in cream. Bring to a gentle boil. Reduce heat to low. Simmer for 3 to 4 minutes or until sauce slightly thickens. Add parsley, parmesan, pasta and reserved cooking liquid. Season with salt and pepper. Toss to combine. Serve.

NUTRITION: (per serve) 2763kJ; 36.4g fat; 22.9g sat fat; 15.1g protein; 66.6g carbs; 3.7g fibre; 101mg chol; 230mg sodium.

FRESH TOMATO & HERB PASTA

SERVES 4   **PREP** 10 minutes   **COOK** 12 minutes

375g dried penne pasta
1 tablespoon olive oil
1 medium red onion, chopped
2 garlic cloves, crushed
1kg ripe tomatoes, chopped
1 teaspoon caster sugar
2 teaspoons white balsamic vinegar
⅓ cup chopped fresh oregano leaves
⅓ cup chopped fresh basil leaves

1 Cook pasta in a large saucepan of boiling salted water, following packet directions, until tender. Drain.

2 Meanwhile, heat oil in a large, deep frying pan over medium heat. Add onion and garlic. Cook for 3 to 4 minutes or until onion has softened. Add tomato, sugar and vinegar. Bring to a simmer. Simmer for 3 to 4 minutes or until slightly thickened. Stir in oregano and basil.

3 Add pasta to tomato mixture. Season with salt and pepper. Toss gently to combine. Serve.

NUTRITION: (per serve) 1744kj; fat 6g; sat fat 0.9g; protein 13.8g; carbs 71.9g; fibre 7.4g; chol 0mg; sodium 96 mg.

Low fat, low kilojoule

TORTELLINI BOSCAIOLA

SERVES 4   **PREP** 15 minutes   **COOK** 15 minutes

625g packet veal tortellini
25g butter
125g shortcut bacon rashers, chopped
1 small brown onion, finely chopped
200g button mushrooms, sliced
4 garlic cloves, crushed
¼ cup dry white wine
300ml thickened cream
2 tablespoons chopped fresh flat-leaf parsley leaves
½ cup finely grated parmesan cheese

1 Cook pasta in a large saucepan of boiling salted water, following packet directions, until tender. Drain, reserving ¼ cup of liquid.

2 Meanwhile, melt butter in a large non-stick frying pan over medium heat. Add bacon, onion and mushrooms. Cook, stirring, for 3 to 4 minutes or until tender. Add garlic. Cook, stirring, for 1 minute or until fragrant. Add white wine. Simmer for 1 minute or until reduced by half.

3 Stir in cream. Bring to a gentle boil. Reduce heat to low. Simmer for 3 to 4 minutes or until sauce slightly thickens. Add parsley, parmesan, pasta and reserved cooking liquid. Season with salt and pepper. Toss to combine. Serve.

NUTRITION: (per serve) 3720kj; fat 53.7g; sat fat 29g; protein 29.5g; carbs 66.2g; fibre 6g; chol 158mg; sodium 1161 mg.

GNOCCHI GORGONZOLA

SERVES 4   **PREP** 10 minutes   **COOK** 10 minutes

500g packet gnocchi
25g butter
4 garlic cloves, crushed
300ml thickened cream
80g gorgonzola cheese, crumbled
⅓ cup finely grated parmesan cheese

1 Cook gnocchi in a saucepan of boiling salted water, following packet directions, until tender. Drain, reserving ¼ cup liquid.

2 Meanwhile, melt butter in a large non-stick frying pan over medium heat. Add garlic. Cook, stirring, for 1 minute or until fragrant.

3 Stir in cream and gorgonzola. Bring to a gentle boil. Reduce heat to low. Simmer for 3 to 4 minutes or until sauce slightly thickens. Add parmesan, gnocchi and reserved cooking liquid. Season with salt and pepper. Toss to combine. Serve.

NUTRITION: (per serve) 2628kj; fat 43.7g; sat fat 26.7g; protein 13.2g; carbs 45.1g; fibre 3.1g; chol 104mg; sodium 1151 mg.

FARFALLE PRIMAVERA

SERVES 4   **PREP** 15 minutes   **COOK** 15 minutes

375g dried farfalle pasta
25g butter
2 zucchini, sliced
4 squash, thickly sliced
4 garlic cloves, crushed
300ml thickened cream
1 tablespoon wholegrain mustard
2 teaspoons finely grated lemon rind
1 cup frozen peas
2 tablespoons chopped flat-leaf parsley leaves
⅓ cup finely grated parmesan cheese

1 Cook pasta in a saucepan of boiling salted water, following packet directions until tender. Drain, reserving ¼ cup liquid.

2 Meanwhile, melt butter in a large non-stick frying pan over medium heat. Add zucchini and squash. Cook, stirring, for 3 to 4 minutes or until tender. Add garlic. Cook, stirring for 1 minute or until fragrant.

3 Stir in cream, mustard and lemon rind. Bring to a gentle boil. Reduce heat to low. Simmer for 3 to 4 minutes or until sauce slightly thickens, adding peas to sauce for the last 2 minutes of simmer time. Add parmesan, pasta and reserved cooking liquid. Season with salt and pepper. Toss to combine. Serve.

NUTRITION: (per serve) 3040kj; fat 37.4g; sat fat 22.9g; protein 20.1g; carbs 73.3g; fibre 9.1g; chol 95mg; sodium 360 mg.

NAPOLETANA SAUCE

SERVES 4

PREP 15 minutes

COOK 45 minutes

1 tablespoon olive oil

1 medium brown onion, finely chopped

2 garlic cloves, crushed

2 tablespoons tomato paste

2 x 400g cans diced tomatoes

1 teaspoon caster sugar

1 tablespoon finely chopped fresh oregano

2 tablespoons finely chopped fresh basil leaves

375g dried penne pasta

1 Heat oil in a saucepan over medium heat. Add onion. Cook, stirring occasionally, for 5 minutes or until onion has softened. Add garlic. Cook for 1 minute or until fragrant.

2 Add tomato paste. Cook, stirring, for 1 minute. Add tomato, ½ cup cold water and sugar.

3 Bring to the boil. Reduce heat to low. Simmer for 20 to 30 minutes or until sauce has slightly thickened. Add oregano and basil. Season with salt and pepper.

4 Meanwhile, cook pasta in a saucepan of boiling salted water, following packet directions, until tender. Drain. Serve sauce tossed through pasta.

NUTRITION: (per serve) 1770kJ; 6.1g fat; 0.8g sat fat; 13g protein; 74.4g carbs; 6.8g fibre; 0mg chol; 250mg sodium.

LINGUINE MARINARA

SERVES 4

PREP 15 minutes

COOK 45 minutes

1 tablespoon olive oil

1 brown onion, finely chopped

2 garlic cloves, crushed

2 tablespoons tomato paste

2 x 400g cans diced tomatoes

½ cup dry white wine

1 teaspoon caster sugar

600g marinara mix

1 tablespoon finely chopped fresh oregano

2 tablespoons finely chopped fresh basil leaves

375g dried linguine

1 Heat oil in a saucepan over medium heat. Add onion. Cook, stirring occasionally, for 5 minutes or until onion has softened. Add garlic. Cook for 1 minute or until fragrant.

2 Add tomato paste. Cook, stirring, for 1 minute. Add tomato, white wine and sugar.

3 Bring to the boil. Reduce heat to low. Simmer for 20 to 30 minutes or until sauce has slightly thickened. Add marinara mix, oregano and basil. Increase heat to medium. Cook for 5 to 6 minutes or until seafood is cooked through. Season with salt and pepper.

4 Meanwhile, cook pasta in a saucepan of boiling salted water, following packet directions, until tender. Drain. Serve sauce tossed through pasta.

NUTRITION: (per serve)2575kj; fat 10.6g; sat fat 2g; protein 44.6g; carbs 75.2g; fibre 6.8g; chol 130mg; sodium 590 mg.

Low fat, high in fibre

SPAGHETTI AMATRICIANA

SERVES 4

PREP 15 minutes

COOK 40 minutes

1 tablespoon olive oil

1 medium brown onion, finely chopped

200g shortcut bacon rashers, trimmed, chopped

2 garlic cloves, crushed

2 long red chillies, seeded, thinly sliced

2 tablespoons tomato paste

2 x 400g cans diced tomatoes

1 teaspoon caster sugar

1 tablespoon finely chopped fresh oregano

2 tablespoons finely chopped fresh basil leaves

375g dried spaghetti

1 Heat oil in a saucepan over medium heat. Add onion and bacon. Cook, stirring occasionally, for 5 minutes or until onion has softened. Add garlic and chilli. Cook for 1 minute or until fragrant.

2 Add tomato paste. Cook, stirring, for 1 minute. Add tomato, ½ cup cold water and sugar.

3 Bring to the boil. Reduce heat to low. Simmer for 20 to 30 minutes or until sauce has slightly thickened. Add oregano and basil. Season with salt and pepper.

4 Meanwhile, cook pasta in a saucepan of boiling salted water, following packet directions, until tender. Drain. Serve sauce tossed through pasta.

NUTRITION: (per serve) 2212kj; fat 14.2g; sat fat 4.1g; protein 20.2g; carbs 75.4g; fibre 7.3g; chol 22mg; sodium 815 mg.

Low fat

AGLIO E OLIO (GARLIC & OIL)

SERVES 4   **PREP** 15 minutes   **COOK** 12 minutes

375g dried spaghettini
⅓ cup extra virgin olive oil
5 garlic cloves, crushed
½ teaspoon dried chilli flakes (optional)
Grated parmesan and finely chopped fresh flat-leaf parsley leaves, to serve

1 Cook pasta in a saucepan of boiling salted water, following packet directions, until tender. Drain, reserving ¼ cup liquid.

2 Heat oil in a large, non-stick frying pan over medium-low heat. Add garlic and chilli, if using. Cook for 1 to 2 minutes or until fragrant. Add pasta and reserved cooking liquid. Season with salt and pepper. Cook, tossing, for 1 to 2 minutes or until combined and heated through. Serve sprinkled with parmesan and parsley.

NUTRITION: (per serve) 2177kJ; 22.2g fat; 4.3g sat fat; 13.5g protein; 64.4g carbs; 3.9g fibre; 7mg chol; 229mg sodium.

EGGPLANT & BACON PASTA

SERVES 4   **PREP** 15 minutes   **COOK** 12 minutes

375g large shell pasta
1 tablespoon olive oil
4 middle bacon rashers, rind removed, thinly sliced
1 large eggplant, cut into 2cm pieces
150g cherry tomatoes, halved
2 garlic cloves, crushed
2 cups tomato pasta sauce
1 cup pitted black olives
½ cup chopped fresh basil leaves
100g fresh ricotta, crumbled
Extra baby basil leaves, to serve

1 Cook pasta in a large saucepan of boiling salted water, following packet directions, until just tender. Drain.

2 Meanwhile, heat oil in a large saucepan over medium-high heat. Add bacon and eggplant. Cook, stirring, for 5 minutes or until bacon is crisp and eggplant is golden. Add tomato and garlic. Cook, stirring, for 1 minute or until fragrant.

3 Add tomato pasta sauce. Bring to the boil. Stir in olives. Reduce heat to low. Simmer, uncovered, for 5 minutes or until eggplant is tender. Add pasta and basil. Gently toss to combine. Serve pasta sprinkled with ricotta and basil leaves.

NUTRITION: (per serve) 2654kJ; 19.4g fat; 6g sat fat; 23.2g protein; 86.8g carbs; 9.2g fibre; 33mg chol; 1435mg sodium.

CHERRY TOMATO & BASIL SPAGHETTI

SERVES 4   **PREP** 10 minutes   **COOK** 16 minutes

375g dried spaghetti
⅓ cup extra virgin olive oil
5 garlic cloves, crushed
400g cherry tomatoes, halved
⅓ cup roughly chopped fresh basil
Grated parmesan, to serve

1 Cook pasta in a saucepan of boiling salted water, following packet directions, until tender. Drain, reserving ¼ cup cooking liquid.

2 Heat oil in a large, non-stick frying pan over medium-low heat. Add garlic and tomato. Cook for 3 to 4 minutes or until tomato is just starting to collapse. Add pasta and reserved liquid. Season with salt and pepper. Cook, tossing, for 1 to 2 minutes or until combined and heated through. Remove from heat. Add basil. Toss to combine. Serve with parmesan.

NUTRITION: (per serve) 2240kj; fat 22.3g; sat fat 4.3g; protein 13.9g; carbs 66.6g; fibre 5.4g; chol 7mg; sodium 190 mg.

Low saturated fat, high in fibre

TUNA & LEMON PASTA

SERVES 4   **PREP** 10 minutes   **COOK** 15 minutes

375g dried shell pasta
⅓ cup extra virgin olive oil
5 garlic cloves, crushed
2 teaspoons finely grated lemon rind
425g can tuna in oil, drained, flaked
2 tablespoons lemon juice
⅓ cup fresh flat-leaf parsley leaves
Grated parmesan, to serve

1 Cook pasta in a saucepan of boiling salted water, following packet directions, until tender. Drain, reserving ¼ cup cooking liquid.

2 Heat oil in a large, non-stick frying pan over medium-low heat. Add garlic and lemon rind. Cook for 1 to 2 minutes or until fragrant. Add pasta, tuna, lemon juice and reserved cooking liquid. Season with salt and pepper. Cook, tossing, for 1 to 2 minutes or until combined and heated through. Sprinkle with parsley. Serve with parmesan.

NUTRITION: (per serve) 2873kj; fat 32.3g; sat fat 5.9g; protein 31.6g; carbs 64.7g; fibre 4g; chol 36mg; sodium 510 mg.

Low saturated fat, lower GI

BROCCOLI, CHILLI & ANCHOVY PASTA

SERVES 4   **PREP** 10 minutes   **COOK** 15 minutes

375g dried spiral pasta
400g broccoli, cut into small florets
⅓ cup extra virgin olive oil
5 garlic cloves, crushed
½ teaspoon dried chilli flakes
4 drained anchovy fillets, finely chopped
Grated parmesan, to serve

1 Cook pasta in a saucepan of boiling salted water, following packet directions, until tender, adding broccoli for the last 4 minutes of cooking. Drain, reserving ¼ cup cooking liquid.

2 Heat oil in a large, non-stick frying pan over medium-low heat. Add garlic, chilli and anchovy. Cook for 1 to 2 minutes or until fragrant. Add pasta, broccoli and reserved cooking liquid. Season with salt and pepper. Cook, tossing, for 1 to 2 minutes or until combined and heated through. Serve with parmesan.

NUTRITION: (per serve) 2338kj; fat 22.8g; sat fat 4.4g; protein 19.1g; carbs 65g; fibre 7.5g; chol 10mg; sodium 320 mg.

Low saturated fat, high in fibre

STOVETOP SPINACH & GARLIC RAVIOLI 'BAKE'

SERVES 4

PREP 15 minutes

COOK 25 minutes (plus 5 minutes standing)

1 tablespoon olive oil

1 brown onion, finely chopped

150g baby spinach

785g bottle tomato, onion and roast garlic pasta sauce

625g packet roast chicken and garlic ravioli

200g mozzarella, sliced

¼ cup fresh basil leaves

1 Heat oil in a 6cm-deep, 24cm heavy-based frying pan over medium heat. Add onion. Cook for 5 minutes or until softened. Add spinach. Cook, stirring, for 2 to 3 minutes or until wilted. Transfer mixture to a sieve set over a bowl. Using the back of a spoon press mixture to drain any excess liquid.

2 Add half the pasta sauce to the pan over low heat. Cook for 1 to 2 minutes or until warmed. Arrange half the ravioli over sauce. Top with spinach mixture, followed by half the mozzarella. Arrange remaining ravioli over mozzarella. Spoon over remaining pasta sauce and top with remaining mozzarella, in a single layer. Season with pepper. Cover. Cook for 15 minutes or until ravioli is cooked and cheese has melted. Stand, uncovered, for 5 minutes. Top with basil leaves. Serve.

NUTRITION: (per serve) 3305kJ; 22.9g fat; 13g sat fat; 41.3g protein; 100.1g carbs; 12g fibre; 45mg chol; 2391mg sodium.

High fibre

BEST-EVER SPAGHETTI CARBONARA

SERVES 4

PREP 10 minutes

COOK 12 minutes

375g dried spaghetti (see note)

1 tablespoon olive oil

200g thick shortcut bacon rashers, halved lengthways, sliced (see note)

3 garlic cloves, crushed

¼ cup dry white wine (optional)

2 eggs

2 egg yolks

½ cup thickened cream

½ cup finely grated parmesan

Extra finely grated parmesan, to serve

1 Cook pasta in a saucepan of boiling salted water, following packet directions, until tender. Drain. Return to saucepan.

2 Meanwhile, heat oil in a frying pan over medium heat. Add bacon. Cook, stirring occasionally, for 5 minutes or until golden. Add garlic. Cook, stirring, for 1 minute or until fragrant. Add wine, if using. Simmer for 1 to 2 minutes or until almost evaporated.

3 Whisk eggs, yolks, cream and parmesan together in a bowl. Season. Add bacon and egg mixtures to pasta in saucepan. Cook, tossing over low heat, for 1 minute until pasta is covered in a creamy, thickened sauce. Serve topped with extra parmesan.

NUTRITION: (per serve) 3062kJ; 36.8g fat; 17.1g sat fat; 30.2g protein; 65.8g carbs; 3.4g fibre; 258mg chol; 973mg sodium.

COOK'S NOTES You could use fettuccine instead of spaghetti. You could also use 200g thinly sliced pancetta, chopped, instead of bacon.

THREE CHEESE PASTA

SERVES 4
PREP 10 minutes
COOK 10 minutes
375g packet fresh lasagne sheets
½ bunch fresh thyme
20g butter
250g tub mascarpone
80g gorgonzola
½ cup finely grated parmesan

1 Using a sharp knife, cut lasagne sheets into 3cm-wide strips.

2 Cook pasta in a saucepan of boiling salted water, following packet directions, until tender. Drain, reserving ¼ cup liquid.

3 Meanwhile, remove thyme leaves from sprigs, reserving any flowers (see note). Melt butter in a large non-stick frying pan over medium heat. Add thyme. Cook for 1 minute or until fragrant. Reduce heat to low. Add mascarpone. Cook, stirring, for 2 to 3 minutes or until melted and smooth. Stir in gorgonzola and parmesan. Cook, stirring, for 1 to 2 minutes or until melted. Add pasta and reserved cooking liquid. Toss for 1 to 2 minutes or until heated through. Season with salt and pepper.

4 Divide pasta between plates. Serve, sprinkled with reserved thyme flowers.

NUTRITION: (per serve) 2768kJ; 44.3g fat; 27g sat fat; 20.1g protein; 44.3g carbs; 5.4g fibre; 92mg chol; 524mg sodium.

COOK'S NOTE Reserve 2 teaspoons thyme sprigs if you don't have flowers.

High fibre, lower sodium

SMOKED SALMON, AVOCADO, LEMON & DILL LINGUINE

SERVES 4
PREP 13 minutes
COOK 12 minutes
375g dried linguine pasta
100g smoked salmon, chopped
1 avocado, roughly chopped
2 tablespoons chopped fresh dill
½ cup pure cream
2 tablespoons grated parmesan cheese
1 tablespoon lemon juice
Extra chopped fresh dill, to serve

1 Cook pasta in a large saucepan of boiling salted water, following packet directions, until tender. Drain. Return to pan.

2 Add salmon, avocado, dill, cream and parmesan to pasta. Cook, tossing, over low heat for 1 to 2 minutes or until heated through. Remove from heat. Stir through lemon juice. Season with salt and pepper. Divide between bowls. Serve topped with extra chopped dill.

NUTRITION: (per serve) 2534kj; fat 28.4g; sat fat 11.7g; protein 19.6g; carbs 65.1g; fibre 4g; chol 47mg; sodium 570 mg.

CREAMY SALMON & BROAD BEAN FETTUCCINE

SERVES 4

PREP 15 minutes

COOK 20 minutes (plus standing time)

400g skinless salmon fillets

375g dried fettuccine

2 cups frozen broad beans

1 tablespoon olive oil

1 small brown onion, finely chopped

1 garlic clove, crushed

¼ cup dry white wine

1 teaspoon finely grated lemon rind

300ml thickened cream

¼ cup roughly chopped fresh chives

1 Fill a medium, deep frying pan two-thirds full with cold water. Add salmon. Bring to the boil over medium-high heat. Reduce heat to low. Simmer, covered, for 5 minutes. Remove from heat. Stand for 5 minutes or until salmon is cooked through. Transfer to a plate. Using a fork, roughly flake salmon.

2 Meanwhile, cook pasta in a saucepan of boiling salted water, following packet directions, until just tender. Drain. Return to saucepan. Place broad beans in a heatproof bowl. Cover with boiling water. Stand for 2 minutes. Drain. Peel and discard skins from broad beans.

3 Heat oil in a large frying pan over medium heat. Add onion and garlic. Cook, stirring, for 5 minutes or until onion has softened. Add wine and lemon rind. Bring to the boil. Add cream and broad beans. Bring to the boil. Reduce heat to low. Cook, stirring occasionally, for 3 to 4 minutes or until sauce thickens slightly. Season with salt and pepper.

4 Add sauce, salmon and chives to pasta. Gently toss over low heat to combine. Serve.

NUTRITION: (per serve) 3287kJ; 26.9g fat; 11.6g sat fat; 50.1g protein; 80.1g carbs; 12.9g fibre; 67 chol; 150mg sodium.

High fibre, lower sodium

ONE-POT SPAGHETTI BOLOGNESE

SERVES 6

PREP 10 minutes

COOK 30 minutes

1 tablespoon extra virgin olive oil

1 brown onion, chopped

1 carrot, finely chopped

1 celery stalk, finely chopped

4 shortcut bacon rashers, trimmed, chopped

2 garlic cloves, finely chopped

600g beef mince

⅓ cup tomato paste

2 x 410g cans crushed tomatoes

3 cups salt-reduced chicken stock

6 sprigs fresh thyme

250g dried spaghetti

¼ cup chopped fresh flat-leaf parsley leaves

Extra chopped fresh flat-leaf parsley leaves and grated parmesan, to serve

1 Heat oil in a large heavy-based flameproof casserole dish or non-stick saucepan over medium-high heat (see note). Add onion, carrot and celery. Cook, stirring occasionally, for 3 minutes or until onion starts to soften. Add bacon. Cook for 3 minutes or until golden. Add garlic. Stir to combine.

2 Add mince to dish. Cook, breaking up mince with a wooden spoon, for 5 minutes or until browned all over. Stir in tomato paste, tomatoes, stock and thyme sprigs. Cover. Bring to the boil. Add spaghetti. Reduce heat to medium. Simmer, uncovered, for 15 minutes or until spaghetti is tender and sauce has thickened, stirring mixture every 5 minutes.

3 Remove pot from heat. Remove and discard thyme sprigs. Add parsley. Season with salt and pepper. Stir to combine. Serve topped with extra chopped parsley and parmesan.

NUTRITION: (per serve) 1966kJ; 16.9g fat; 6.6g sat fat; 36.2g protein; 40.4g carbs; 5.6g fibre; 81mg chol; 1097mg sodium.

COOK'S NOTE We used a cast-iron dish for this recipe to prevent the sauce from sticking to the base.

High fibre

CREAMY CHICKEN, PEA & SPINACH PENNE

SERVES 4

PREP 10 minutes

COOK 20 minutes

1 tablespoon extra virgin olive oil

1 red onion, thinly sliced

2 tablespoons tomato paste

250g cherry tomatoes, halved

1½ 2 cups chicken stock

3 cups dried penne

⅔ cup frozen peas

½ cup thickened cream

2 tablespoons wholegrain mustard

2 cups shredded cooked chicken

80g baby spinach

¼ cup chopped fresh flat-leaf parsley leaves

1 Heat oil in a large heavy-based saucepan or flameproof casserole dish over medium-high heat (see note). Add onion. Cook, stirring, for 5 minutes. Add tomato paste, tomato, stock and 1½ cups cold water. Cover. Bring to the boil.

cook penne separately

2 ~~Add~~ penne. Bring to the boil. Reduce heat to medium. Simmer, uncovered, stirring occasionally, for 15 minutes or until pasta is tender and sauce has almost thickened, adding peas in the last 2 minutes of cooking. Season with salt and pepper. Stir in cream, mustard and half the chicken. Remove from heat.

3 Stir in spinach. Serve topped with remaining chicken and parsley.

NUTRITION: (per serve) 2961kJ; 23.8g fat; 9.9g sat fat; 35.1g protein; 83.5g carbs; 8.5g fibre; 96mg chol; 1065mg sodium.

COOK'S NOTE We used a cast-iron pot for this recipe to prevent the sauce from sticking to the base. You could use a heavy-based non-stick pan if preferred.

High fibre

PUMPKIN, BROCCOLI & BACON PASTA

SERVES 4

PREP 10 minutes

COOK 20 minutes

1 tablespoon extra virgin olive oil

1 red onion, halved, sliced

6 shortcut bacon rashers, trimmed, chopped

500g butternut pumpkin, peeled, cut into 2cm cubes

2 garlic cloves, thinly sliced

4 sprigs fresh thyme

1 cup chicken stock

250g dried spaghetti (see note)

1 head broccoli, cut into small florets

¼ cup thickened cream

Toasted pine nuts, fresh basil leaves and finely grated
   parmesan, to serve

1 Heat oil in a large heavy-based saucepan or flameproof casserole dish over medium-high heat. Add onion, bacon and pumpkin. Cook, stirring occasionally, for 5 minutes or until onion is softened. Add garlic and thyme. Stir to combine.

2 Add chicken stock and 2 cups cold water. Cover. Bring to the boil. Add spaghetti. Reduce heat to medium. Simmer, uncovered, for 10 minutes, stirring occasionally. Add broccoli. Simmer for 5 minutes, stirring occasionally, or until pasta and broccoli are tender and the sauce has thickened.

3 Remove from heat. Remove and discard the thyme sprigs. Stir in cream. Season with salt and pepper. Serve pasta sprinkled with pine nuts, basil leaves and parmesan.

NUTRITION: (per serve) 2370kJ; 26.6g fat; 9.4g sat fat; 22.4g protein; 58.7g carbs; 7.2g fibre; 67mg chol; 1037mg sodium.

COOK'S NOTE Many different sorts of pastas would work with this sauce. Try using linguine or farfalle instead of spaghetti.

High fibre

TOMATO, BACON & OLIVE LINGUINE

SERVES 4
PREP 10 minutes
COOK 20 minutes

1 tablespoon extra virgin olive oil
1 red onion, thinly sliced
6 shortcut bacon rashers, trimmed, chopped
3 garlic cloves, thinly sliced
2 tablespoons tomato paste
2 cups salt-reduced chicken stock
250g dried linguine
250g cherry tomatoes, halved
¼ cup basil pesto
¾ cup mixed olives
40g baby rocket
Shaved parmesan, to serve

1 Heat oil in a large heavy-based saucepan or flameproof casserole dish over medium-high heat. Add onion and bacon. Cook, stirring, for 5 minutes or until onion is softened. Add garlic. Stir to combine. Add tomato paste, stock and 1 cup cold water. Cover. Bring to the boil.

2 Add linguine. Bring to the boil. Reduce heat to medium. Simmer, uncovered, for 15 minutes or until pasta is just tender and sauce has thickened, stirring every 5 minutes.

3 Remove from heat. Stir in tomato, pesto and olives. Season with pepper. Serve topped with baby rocket and parmesan.

NUTRITION: (per serve) 2029kJ; 18.5g fat; 5.5g sat fat; 20g protein; 56.8g carbs; 5g fibre; 48mg chol; 1572mg sodium.

ASPARAGUS, SNOW PEA & LEMON RISONI

SERVES 4
PREP 10 minutes
COOK 25 minutes

1 tablespoon extra virgin olive oil
1 brown onion, chopped
3 garlic cloves, crushed
⅓ cup dry white wine
3 cups chicken stock
1⅔ cups dried risoni pasta
2 bunches asparagus, trimmed, cut into 4cm lengths
150g snow peas, trimmed, halved
¼ cup lemon juice
¼ cup chopped fresh flat-leaf parsley leaves
100g fetta, crumbled
2 teaspoons finely grated lemon rind

1 Heat oil in a heavy-based saucepan or flameproof casserole dish over medium-high heat. Add onion. Cook, stirring, for 5 minutes or until softened. Add garlic. Cook for 1 minute. Add wine. Simmer until almost evaporated. Stir in stock and 1½ cups cold water. Cover. Bring to the boil.

2 Add risoni to stock mixture. Bring to the boil. Reduce the heat to medium. Simmer, uncovered, for 15 minutes or until risoni is just tender and liquid is almost absorbed, stirring every 5 minutes. Add the asparagus and snow peas 2 minutes before the end of cooking time.

3 Stir in lemon juice and chopped flat-leaf parsley. Season with salt and pepper. Serve sprinkled with fetta and lemon rind.

NUTRITION: (per serve) 2164kJ; 11.8g fat; 4.7g sat fat; 22.4g protein; 72g carbs; 6.6g fibre; 16mg chol; 1333mg sodium.

High fibre

RICH TOMATO, SALAMI & CHARGRILLED VEGETABLE RIGATONI

SERVES 4
PREP 5 minutes
COOK 25 minutes

1 tablespoon extra virgin olive oil
1 red onion, thinly sliced
150g cup mushrooms, sliced
150g Danish salami, torn
1½ cups tomato passata
2 tablespoons tomato paste
3 cups salt-reduced chicken stock
2 fresh rosemary sprigs
250g dried rigatoni
280g jar antipasto, drained
¼ cup fresh basil leaves
Grated parmesan and garlic bread, to serve

1 Heat oil in a large heavy-based saucepan or flameproof casserole dish. Add onion. Cook, stirring, for 2 minutes. Add mushrooms and salami. Cook, stirring, for 3 minutes. Add passata, tomato paste, stock and rosemary. Stir well to combine. Cover. Bring to the boil.

2 Add rigatoni. Bring to the boil. Reduce heat to medium. Simmer, uncovered, for 20 minutes or until pasta is tender and sauce has thickened, stirring every 5 minutes. Season with salt and pepper. Remove and discard rosemary.

3 Stir in antipasto. Top with basil and parmesan. Serve with garlic bread.

NUTRITION: (per serve) 2435kJ; 27g fat; 7.7g sat fat; 24g protein; 57.3g carbs; 7g fibre; 52mg chol; 1707mg sodium.

High fibre

SMOKED SALMON & SNOW PEA PASTA SALAD

SERVES 4
PREP 10 minutes
COOK 12 minutes

375g dried penne pasta
200g snow peas, trimmed, halved
⅓ cup creamy roasted garlic dressing
200g smoked salmon, torn
1 bunch radish, trimmed, sliced
¼ cup fresh dill sprigs

1 Cook pasta in a large saucepan of boiling salted water, following packet directions, until tender, adding snow peas in the last 1 minute of cooking time. Drain. Rinse under cold water. Drain well. Transfer to a large bowl.

2 Combine dressing and 2 tablespoons cold water in a small bowl.

3 Add smoked salmon, radish and dill to pasta mixture. Drizzle dressing over pasta mixture. Season with salt and pepper. Toss gently to combine. Serve.

NUTRITION: (per serve) 2013kJ; 7.7g fat; 0.9g sat fat; 23.9g protein; 75.7g carbs; 4.6g fibre; 28mg chol; 1056mg sodium.

Low fat, lower GI

SPAGHETTI WITH PEA PESTO & CRISPY BACON

SERVES 4
PREP 15 minutes
COOK 13 minutes

400g dried wholegrain spaghetti
½ x 350g jar marinated fetta
500g packet frozen peas
1 garlic clove, chopped
⅓ cup chopped fresh basil leaves
⅓ cup grated parmesan
4 middle bacon rashers, trimmed, thinly sliced

1 Cook pasta in a large saucepan of boiling salted water, following packet directions, until tender. Drain, reserving ⅓ cup of cooking liquid. Return pasta to saucepan.

2 Drain fetta, reserving 2 tablespoons oil. Crumble fetta.

3 Cook peas, following packet directions, until just tender. Drain. Place 2 cups of the peas in a food processor or blender. Add garlic, basil, parmesan and reserved oil. Process until almost smooth.

4 Cook bacon in a medium frying pan over medium heat for 3 to 4 minutes or until browned and crisp. Add pesto, bacon, remaining peas and reserved cooking liquid to pasta. Season with pepper. Toss to combine. Serve pasta topped with fetta.

NUTRITION: (per serve) 2963kJ; 25.4g fat; 9.5g sat fat; 34.9g protein; 79g carbs; 10.8g fibre; 33mg chol; 1077mg sodium.

COOK'S NOTE Add any excess oil in pan from cooking the bacon to the pasta mixture for added flavour.

High fibre

VEAL TORTELLINI WITH ROAST CAPSICUM SAUCE

SERVES 4
PREP 5 minutes
COOK 10 minutes

450g jar whole fire-roasted peeled peppers, drained
2 medium tomatoes, chopped
½ teaspoon dried marjoram
1 tablespoon olive oil
2 garlic cloves, chopped
625g packet veal tortellini
2 tablespoons fresh basil leaves
Grated parmesan, to serve

1 Place peppers, tomato, marjoram, oil, garlic and 1 cup cold water in a food processor or blender. Process until smooth.

2 Transfer tomato mixture to a large saucepan. Place over medium-high heat. Bring to a simmer. Add tortellini. Season with salt and pepper. Cover. Cook for 5 to 7 minutes, stirring occasionally, or until tortellini is tender.

3 Serve pasta topped with basil and parmesan.

NUTRITION: (per serve) 2364kJ; 17.6g fat; 7.2g sat fat; 23.5g protein; 76.4g carbs; 6g fibre; 47mg chol; 1494mg sodium.

High fibre

CREAMY MUSHROOM PAPPARDELLE WITH PISTACHIO GREMOLATA

SERVES 4
PREP 20 minutes
COOK 12 minutes

225g dried pappardelle pasta
1 tablespoon olive oil
1 large red onion, halved, thinly sliced
1 shortcut bacon rasher, thinly sliced
375g flat mushrooms, sliced
2 garlic cloves, crushed
2 teaspoons finely chopped fresh rosemary leaves
250ml tub extra light cream for cooking
1 bunch English spinach, trimmed, leaves torn in half
Pistachio gremolata
⅓ cup unsalted roasted pistachio kernels, finely chopped
½ cup fresh flat-leaf parsley leaves, finely chopped
2 teaspoons finely grated lemon rind
1 tablespoon drained baby capers, rinsed, finely chopped

1 Make Pistachio gremolata Place all ingredients in a bowl. Stir to combine. Set aside.

2 Cook pasta in a large saucepan of boiling salted water, following packet directions, until just tender. Drain, reserving ¼ cup cooking liquid.

3 Meanwhile, heat oil in a large, deep frying pan over high heat. Add onion and bacon. Cook, stirring, for 5 minutes or until onion has softened and is starting to brown. Add mushrooms, garlic and rosemary. Cook, stirring occasionally, for 3 minutes or until softened. Reduce heat to low. Stir in cream until well combined and smooth. Simmer gently for 2 minutes.

4 Remove pan from heat. Add spinach, reserved cooking liquid and pasta. Toss gently to combine. Season with salt and pepper. Serve sprinkled with pistachio gremolata.

NUTRITION: (per serve) 1933kJ; 15.8g fat; 4.2g sat fat; 18.5g protein; 55g carbs; 9g fibre; 9mg chol; 425mg sodium.

High in fibre, heart friendly, low saturated fat

CRAB, LEMON & HERB LINGUINE

SERVES 4
PREP 15 minutes
COOK 15 minutes

375g dried linguine pasta
1 tablespoon olive oil
3 garlic cloves, crushed
1 long red chilli, thinly sliced
225g tub fresh crab meat
½ cup crème fraîche
¼ cup lemon juice
⅓ cup finely chopped fresh basil leaves
⅓ cup finely chopped fresh flat-leaf parsley leaves
Lemon wedges, to serve

1 Cook pasta in a large saucepan of boiling salted water, following packet directions, until tender. Drain, reserving ½ cup cooking liquid.

2 Heat oil in a large saucepan over high heat. Add garlic and chilli. Cook, stirring, for 1 minute or until fragrant. Add crab, cooking liquid and cream. Cook for 1 to 2 minutes or until heated through. Add pasta, lemon juice, basil and parsley. Season. Toss to coat. Serve with lemon.

NUTRITION: (per serve) 2021kJ; 13.6g fat; 6.2g sat fat; 19.5g protein; 67g carbs; 4g fibre; 56mg chol; 405mg sodium.

Low fat, lower sodium

SPICY TUNA PASTA SALAD

SERVES 4   **PREP** 5 minutes   **COOK** 10 minutes

250g dried linguine pasta
2 x 185g cans tuna in chilli and oil
400g can artichoke hearts in brine, drained, quartered
50g baby rocket
1 avocado, chopped
2 tablespoons lemon juice

1 Cook pasta in a large saucepan of boiling salted water, following packet directions, until tender. Drain. Rinse under cold water. Drain well.

2 Place pasta in a large bowl. Drain tuna, reserving oil. Remove and discard chilli. Flake tuna into large chunks. Add tuna, reserved oil, artichokes, rocket and avocado to pasta. Drizzle with lemon juice. Season well with salt and pepper. Gently toss to combine. Serve.

NUTRITION: (per serve) 2441kJ; 19.9g fat; 4.4g sat fat; 30.3g protein; 66g carbs; 6.7g fibre; 20mg chol; 600mg sodium.

Low saturated fat, high fibre, lower GI

GARLIC CHILLI PRAWN PASTA

SERVES 4   **PREP** 3 minutes   **COOK** 12 minutes

200g dried angel hair pasta
⅓ cup extra virgin olive oil
4 garlic cloves, crushed
1 teaspoon dried chilli flakes
1 teaspoon sea salt
400g peeled, tails intact, medium green prawns
¼ cup lemon juice
¼ cup finely chopped fresh flat-leaf parsley leaves
Extra virgin olive oil, to serve

1 Cook angel hair pasta in a large saucepan of boiling salted water, following packet directions, until tender. Drain.

2 Meanwhile, heat olive oil in a large, deep frying pan over medium-high heat. Add garlic, chilli flakes and salt. Cook, stirring, for 1 to 2 minutes or until fragrant. Add prawns. Cook, stirring, for 3 to 4 minutes or until prawns turn pink and are almost cooked through.

3 Add pasta, lemon juice and parsley to pan. Cook, tossing, for 1 minute or until combined and prawns are cooked through. Serve drizzled with extra virgin olive oil.

NUTRITION: (per serve)1842kj; fat 24.4g; sat fat 3.5g; protein 18.8g; carbs 34.9g; fibre 2.4g; chol 93mg; sodium 717 mg.

Low saturated fat, lower GI

CHILLI PRAWN & BASIL PASTA

SERVES 4
PREP 20 minutes
COOK 15 minutes

20 (1kg) medium green king prawns
375g dried linguine pasta
2 tablespoons extra virgin olive oil
1 small red onion, halved, thinly sliced
2 garlic cloves, crushed
½ teaspoon dried chilli flakes
400g can Italian cherry tomatoes in tomato juice
½ cup salt-reduced chicken stock
1 teaspoon caster sugar
¼ cup shredded fresh basil leaves
Fresh basil leaves, to serve

1 Peel and devein prawns, leaving tails intact.

2 Cook pasta in a large saucepan of boiling salted water, following packet directions, until tender. Drain.

3 Meanwhile, heat oil in a large, deep frying pan over medium heat. Add onion. Cook, stirring, for 3 to 4 minutes or until onion has softened. Add garlic and chilli. Cook for 1 minute or until fragrant. Add tomatoes, stock and sugar. Bring to a simmer. Simmer for 5 minutes. Add prawns. Simmer for 5 minutes or until prawns are cooked through and tomato mixture has thickened slightly. Stir in basil.

4 Add pasta to tomato mixture. Season with salt and pepper. Toss to combine. Serve sprinkled with fresh basil leaves.

NUTRITION: (per serve) 2279kJ; 11.2g fat; 1.6g sat fat; 37.8g protein; 69.6g carbs; 4.9g fibre; 187mg chol; 645mg sodium.

Lower GI, low fat

BEEF

GINGER BEEF STIR-FRY

SERVES 4   **PREP** 15 minutes   **COOK** 10 minutes

500g beef stir-fry strips
4cm piece fresh ginger, peeled, cut into matchsticks
¼ cup light soy sauce
2 tablespoons peanut oil
250g mixed mushrooms, sliced
200g sugar snap peas, trimmed
1 bunch Chinese broccoli, stems finely chopped,
    leaves torn
5 green onions, trimmed, thinly sliced
440g thin egg-style noodles
1½ tablespoons shao hsing (Chinese cooking wine)

1 Combine beef, ginger and 2 tablespoons soy sauce
in a medium bowl. Toss to coat. Heat a wok over high
heat. Add 2 teaspoons oil. Swirl to coat. Add ⅓ of the
beef mixture. Stir-fry for 1 minute or until browned.
Transfer to bowl. Add 2 teaspoons remaining oil. Swirl
to coat. Add half the remaining beef mixture. Stir-fry
for 1 minute or until browned. Transfer to bowl.
Repeat with 2 teaspoons remaining oil and beef.

2 Add remaining oil to wok. Swirl to coat. Add
mushrooms. Stir-fry for 2 minutes or until tender.
Transfer to bowl. Add sugar snap peas. Stir-fry for
2 minutes. Add broccoli stems and two-thirds of onion.
Stir-fry for 1 minute or until peas are bright green and
lightly charred. Return beef and mushrooms to wok.
Add noodles, broccoli leaves, wine and remaining soy.

Stir-fry for 1 to 2 minutes or until hot and leaves have
wilted. Sprinkle with remaining onion. Serve.

NUTRITION: (per serve) 2985kJ; 13.6g fat; 3.1g sat fat; 54.7g
protein; 83.9g carbs; 8.9g fibre; 87mg chol; 1088mg sodium.

High fibre, low saturated fat

ALMOND & SAGE VEAL SCHNITZELS

SERVES 4   **PREP** 15 minutes   **COOK** 10 minutes

½ cup plain flour
⅓ cup milk
2 eggs
1½ cups fresh breadcrumbs
½ cup flaked almonds
1 tablespoon finely chopped fresh sage leaves
1 teaspoon finely grated lemon rind
4 x 100g veal schnitzels (uncrumbed)
Rice bran oil, for shallow-frying
Steamed baby red delight potatoes, green beans and
    lemon wedges, to serve

1 Place flour on a plate. Place milk and egg in a shallow
bowl. Whisk until combined. Combine breadcrumbs,
almonds, sage and lemon rind on a plate.

2 Coat 1 piece veal in flour, shaking off excess. Dip
in egg mixture. Coat in breadcrumb mixture. Place
on a tray. Repeat with remaining veal, flour, egg and
breadcrumb mixtures (see note).

3 Pour enough oil into a large frying pan to come
5mm up side of pan. Heat over medium-high heat.
Cook veal for 2 minutes each side or until just cooked
through. Transfer to a plate lined with paper towel to
drain. Serve schnitzels with steamed potatoes, beans
and lemon wedges.

NUTRITION: (per serve) 2377kJ; 21.7g fat; 4.5g sat fat; 37.3g
protein; 51g carbs; 7.7g fibre; 179mg chol; 295mg sodium.

COOK'S NOTE This crumb mixture also works well with
lamb or pork cutlets; or try sprinkling over fish fillets
before baking.

Low saturated fat, heart friendly, high fibre

EASY VEAL PARMIGIANA

SERVES 4   **PREP** 10 minutes   **COOK** 15 minutes

400g eggplant, thinly sliced lengthways
⅓ cup olive oil
375g dried pappardelle pasta
4 (110g each) veal schnitzels, uncrumbed
1 cup napoletana pasta sauce
5 bocconcini, each cut into 3 slices

1 Heat a chargrill pan over medium-high heat. Brush eggplant with 2 tablespoons oil. Cook eggplant, in batches, for 4 minutes each side or until charred and tender.

2 Cook pasta in a large saucepan of boiling salted water, following packet directions, until tender. Drain. Transfer to a heatproof bowl. Add 1 tablespoon oil. Toss to coat.

3 Meanwhile, season veal. Heat 2 teaspoons oil in a frying pan over high heat. Cook half the veal for 30 seconds each side or until golden. Transfer to a plate. Repeat with 2 teaspoons oil and remaining veal. Arrange half the eggplant in an ovenproof dish. Top with veal and remaining eggplant. Spoon over sauce. Arrange cheese over sauce. Preheat grill on high. Grill for 3 to 5 minutes or until cheese is melted. Serve veal with pasta.

NUTRITION: (per serve) 3251kJ; 30.8g fat; 8.6g sat fat; 46.6g protein; 74.5g carbs; 8g fibre; 108mg chol; 583mg sodium.

high fibre, lower sodium

MEXICAN BEEF & CORN RISSOLES WITH TORTILLAS

SERVES 4   **PREP** 20 minutes   **COOK** 10 minutes

500g beef mince
410g can creamed corn
¾ cup dried panko breadcrumbs
30g taco spice mix
1 cup grated tasty cheese
1 cup roughly chopped fresh coriander leaves
1 tablespoon olive oil
425g can Mexe-beans
8 flour tortillas, warmed
1 large avocado, sliced
½ cup sour cream
Lime wedges, to serve

1 Combine mince, corn, breadcrumbs, spice mix, ⅓ cup cheese and ⅓ cup coriander in a large bowl. Season with pepper. Using damp hands, shape 1½ tablespoons of mixture, 1 at a time, into 32 rissoles.

2 Heat oil in a large non-stick frying pan over medium-high heat. Cook rissoles for 2 minutes each side. Reduce heat to medium. Cook for a further 4 minutes, each side or until cooked through.

3 Meanwhile, place beans in a small heatproof bowl. Microwave on MEDIUM (50%) for 3 to 4 minutes or until heated through. Drain.

4 Place tortillas on a flat surface. Top with beans, rissoles, avocado and a dollop of sour cream. Sprinkle with remaining cheese and coriander. Fold tortillas to enclose filling. Serve with lime wedges.

NUTRITION: (per serve) 4932kJ; 63.9g fat; 26.6g sat fat; 54.1g protein; 89.4g carbs; 13.8g fibre; 140mg chol; 2317mg sodium.

High fibre

CLASSIC STEAK DIANE

SERVES 4

PREP 10 minutes

COOK 20 minutes

750g chat potatoes

1 bunch broccolini, trimmed

1 carrot, cut into thick batons

4 (150g each) beef rump steaks

80g butter, chopped

2 teaspoons worcestershire sauce

¼ cup salt-reduced beef stock

1 garlic clove, finely chopped

2 tablespoons finely chopped fresh flat-leaf
  parsley leaves

2 tablespoons chopped fresh chives

1 Place potatoes in a metal steamer. Place steamer in a large saucepan of simmering water. Cook, covered, for 15 minutes or until almost tender. Add broccolini and carrot. Cook, covered, for 4 to 5 minutes or until tender.

2 Meanwhile, season steaks with salt and pepper. Melt 1 tablespoon butter in a large frying pan over high heat until golden. Add steak. Cook, for 2 minutes each side for medium, or until cooked to your liking. Transfer to a large plate. Cover loosely with foil. Rest for 5 minutes.

3 Add worcestershire sauce, stock and garlic to pan over medium-high heat. Bring to the boil. Reduce heat to low. Simmer for 2 minutes. Remove from heat. Add remaining butter. Whisk until melted and sauce has thickened slightly. Stir in parsley and chives. Serve steaks with sauce and steamed vegetables.

NUTRITION: (per serve) 2125kJ; 23.9g fat; 14g sat fat; 39.7g protein; 30.7g carbs; 6g fibre; 147mg chol; 345mg sodium.

High fibre, lower sodium

CHARGRILLED STEAK & ANTIPASTO SALAD

SERVES 4

PREP 10 minutes

COOK 15 minutes

500g beef rump steak

1 tablespoon dried oregano leaves

2 tablespoons olive oil

2 red capsicums, cut into 3cm-thick slices

270g jar antipasto

1 baby cos lettuce

½ loaf crusty bread, sliced

1 Place steak on a large plate. Sprinkle with oregano and season well with salt and pepper, pressing to secure. Drizzle with half the oil.

2 Preheat a barbecue hot plate or chargrill on medium-high heat. Place capsicum in a bowl. Add remaining oil. Season with salt and pepper. Toss to coat. Cook capsicum, turning occasionally, for 4 minutes or until charred and tender. Transfer to a heatproof bowl.

3 Add steak to barbecue hot plate or chargrill. Cook for 3 to 4 minutes each side, for medium, or until cooked to your liking. Transfer to a plate. Cover loosely with foil. Set aside for 5 minutes to rest. Slice.

4 Meanwhile, drain antipasto, reserving 1½ tablespoons of the oil. Add antipasto and reserved oil to capsicum strips. Toss to combine. Place lettuce on a platter. Top with chargrilled capsicum mixture and steak. Serve with crusty bread.

NUTRITION: (per serve) 1807kJ; 20.4g fat; 4.8g sat fat; 33.3g protein; 27.1g carbs; 3.9g fibre; 80mg chol; 677mg sodium.

Low saturated fat

AMERICAN-STYLE BEEF BURGERS

SERVES 4

PREP 30 minutes

COOK 10 minutes

500g beef mince

1 small brown onion, finely chopped

1 garlic clove, crushed

1 tablespoon worcestershire sauce

2 tablespoons American mustard

2 teaspoons olive oil

4 slices gouda cheese

4 hamburger buns, split, toasted

2 tablespoons tomato sauce

¼ cup bread and butter cucumbers

Salad slaw

3 cups shredded iceberg lettuce

1 carrot, peeled, grated

1 small red onion, halved, thinly sliced

125g cherry tomatoes, halved

¼ cup mayonnaise

2 tablespoons French dressing

1 Place mince, onion and garlic in a large bowl. Season with pepper. Add worcestershire sauce and 1 tablespoon mustard to mince mixture. Mix to combine. Shape into four 1.5cm-thick patties.

2 Heat oil in a large, non-stick frying pan over medium heat. Cook patties for 5 minutes each side or until cooked through. Top each patty with 1 cheese slice. Place patties on bun bases. Top with remaining mustard, tomato sauce and cucumber. Sandwich with bun tops.

3 Make Salad slaw Place lettuce, carrot, red onion and tomato in a bowl. Combine mayonnaise and dressing in a bowl. Drizzle over salad. Toss. Serve burgers with salad.

NUTRITION: (per serve) 2907kJ; 30.2g fat; 11.4g sat fat; 44.7g protein; 55.4g carbs; 5.4g fibre; 98mg chol; 1441mg sodium.

CREAMY MUSTARD VEAL WITH PAPPARDELLE

SERVES 4
PREP 15 minutes
COOK 20 minutes

1 tablespoon olive oil
375g cherry truss tomatoes
225g dried pappardelle pasta
¼ cup plain flour
8 (650g) thin veal escalopes
50g butter
⅔ cup dry white wine
⅔ cup crème fraîche
⅓ cup pure cream
1 tablespoon wholegrain mustard
1 tablespoon finely chopped fresh chives
Steamed green beans, to serve

1 Heat oil in a large frying pan over medium heat. Add tomatoes. Cook for 5 minutes or until skins start to split. Transfer to a plate. Cover to keep warm.

2 Cook pasta in a large saucepan of boiling salted water, following packet directions, until tender. Drain. Cover to keep warm.

3 Meanwhile, place flour on a large plate. Dust both sides of veal lightly in flour. Melt half the butter in pan over medium-high heat. Add half the veal. Cook for 1 to 2 minutes each side for medium, or until cooked to your liking. Remove from pan. Cover to keep warm. Repeat with remaining butter and veal.

4 Add wine to pan and cook for 3 to 4 minutes or until reduced by half. Add crème fraîche, cream and mustard. Simmer for 2 to 3 minutes or until thickened slightly. Stir in chives. Serve veal with pasta, sauce, tomatoes and beans.

NUTRITION: (per serve) 3379kj; fat 43g; sat fat 23.6g; protein 45.3g; carbs 50g; fibre 5.4g; chol 193mg; sodium 390 mg.

STEAK SANDWICH SALAD

SERVES 4
PREP 15 minutes
COOK 10 minutes (plus 5 minutes standing time)
6 slices Italian-style bread
Olive oil cooking spray
500g beef rump steak
100g mixed salad leaves
1 small red onion, halved, thinly sliced
2 medium tomatoes, cut into thin wedges
425g can baby beetroot, drained, quartered
Toasted walnuts (optional)
Creamy tarragon dressing
¼ cup dijonnaise
1½ teaspoons chopped fresh tarragon

1 Heat a chargrill pan over medium heat. Spray both sides of bread with oil. Cook bread slices for 1 minute each side or until golden. Tear bread into 4 to 6 pieces.

2 Spray steak with oil. Season with salt and pepper. Cook steak for 3 to 4 minutes each side for medium or until cooked to your liking. Transfer to a plate. Cover with foil. Rest for 5 minutes. Thinly slice.

3 Combine bread, steak, salad leaves, onion, tomato and beetroot in a large bowl. Toss to combine.

4 **Make Creamy tarragon dressing** Place dijonnaise, tarragon and 2 tablespoons cold water in a screw-top jar. Shake to combine.

5 Drizzle dijonnaise mixture over salad. Toss gently to combine. Serve. Add toasted walnuts for crunch.

NUTRITION: (per serve) 2065kj; fat 15.1g; sat fat 3.9g; protein 35.9g; carbs 51.1g; fibre 5.5g; chol 80mg; sodium 941 mg.

High fibre

CHEAT'S MOUSSAKA

SERVES 6

PREP 15 minutes

COOK 30 minutes

1 large eggplant, thinly sliced

Olive oil cooking spray

1 tablespoon olive oil

1 medium brown onion, finely chopped

2 garlic cloves, crushed

800g beef mince

1 teaspoon ground cinnamon

½ teaspoon ground allspice

2 x 400g cans crushed tomatoes

200g plain Greek-style yoghurt

1 cup grated tasty cheese

Ground cinnamon, extra, salad leaves and lemon
   wedges, to serve

1 Spray eggplant with oil. Heat a large frying pan over medium-high heat. Cook eggplant, in batches, for 2 to 3 minutes each side or until browned. Transfer to a chopping board. Roughly chop.

2 Meanwhile, heat oil in a saucepan over medium-high heat. Add onion and garlic. Cook, stirring, for 5 minutes or until onion has softened. Add mince. Cook, stirring with a wooden spoon to break up mince, for 6 minutes or until browned. Add cinnamon and allspice. Cook, stirring, for 30 seconds or until fragrant. Add tomato. Bring to the boil. Reduce heat to medium-low. Simmer for 15 minutes or until sauce has thickened.

3 Preheat grill on high. Add eggplant to mince mixture. Stir to combine. Spoon mixture into an 8 cup-capacity ovenproof dish. Spread yoghurt over mince mixture. Sprinkle with cheese. Grill for 3 minutes or until cheese is golden. Sprinkle with extra cinnamon and serve with salad leaves and lemon wedges.

NUTRITION: (per serve)1854kj; fat 24.8g; sat fat 11.6g; protein 39.1g; carbs 13.3g; fibre 5.5g; chol 100mg; sodium 633 mg.

High fibre

STEAK BOURGUIGNON

SERVES 4
PREP 15 minutes
COOK 25 minutes

50g butter
2 eschalots, finely chopped
2 rashers shortcut bacon, thinly sliced
2 garlic cloves, crushed
1 tablespoon plain flour
½ cup red wine
1 cup beef stock
4 x 150g beef scotch fillet steaks
Olive oil cooking spray
100g button mushrooms, thinly sliced
Mashed potato and steamed green beans, to serve

1 Melt half the butter in a saucepan over medium heat. Add eschalot, bacon and garlic. Cook, stirring, for 5 minutes or until onion has softened. Add flour. Cook, stirring, for 1 minute. Gradually add wine, stirring constantly. Bring to the boil. Add stock. Reduce heat to low. Simmer for 15 minutes or until slightly thickened. Season with salt and pepper.

2 Meanwhile, season steaks with salt and pepper. Spray a large frying pan with oil. Heat over high heat. Cook steaks for 3 to 4 minutes each side for medium or until cooked to your liking. Transfer to a plate. Cover to keep warm.

3 Melt remaining butter in pan over high heat. Add mushrooms. Cook for 5 minutes or until golden. Spoon mashed potato onto plates. Top with steaks and mushrooms. Spoon over red wine mixture. Serve with beans.

NUTRITION: (per serve) 2216kj; fat 26.1g; sat fat 14.1g; protein 40.4g; carbs 25.2g; fibre 4.8g; chol 134mg; sodium 773 mg.

High in iron

EASY BEEF MASSAMAN CURRY

SERVES 4

PREP 6 minutes

COOK 25 minutes

2 teaspoons vegetable oil

1 brown onion, finely chopped

500g extra-lean beef mince

2 tablespoons massaman curry paste

375ml can coconut-flavoured evaporated milk

1 tablespoon brown sugar

2 cups frozen mixed vegetables (see note)

¼ cup fresh coriander leaves

Steamed jasmine rice, to serve

1 Heat oil in a large non-stick frying pan over medium heat. Add the onion. Cook, stirring occasionally, for 5 minutes or until softened.

2 Add mince. Cook, breaking up mince with a wooden spoon, for 5 minutes or until browned. Add curry paste. Cook for 1 minute or until fragrant. Add evaporated milk. Bring to a simmer. Stir in the sugar. Reduce heat to medium-low. Cook for 5 minutes or until thickened slightly.

3 Add frozen vegetables. Cook, covered, for 4 to 5 minutes or until vegetables are just tender. Serve curry on rice sprinkled with coriander leaves.

NUTRITION: (per serve) 2041kJ; 15g fat; 5.3g sat fat; 39.1g protein; 46.9g carbs; 3.2g fibre; 72mg chol; 385mg sodium.

COOK'S NOTE We used a packet mix of frozen vegetables from the supermarket that included baby beans, carrot and baby corn.

Low saturated fat, lower sodium

BEEF STROGANOFF

SERVES 4

PREP 15 minutes

COOK 15 minutes

250g dried fettuccine

1 tablespoon olive oil

600g rump steak, thinly sliced

20g butter

1 large brown onion, thinly sliced

2 garlic cloves, crushed

200g button mushrooms, thinly sliced

1 tablespoon paprika

1 cup sour cream

½ cup beef stock

1 tablespoon lemon juice

2 tablespoons finely chopped fresh chives

1 Cook fettuccine in a saucepan of boiling salted water, following packet directions, until tender. Drain.

2 Meanwhile, heat oil in a large, deep frying pan over medium-high heat. Cook beef, in batches, for 2 to 3 minutes or until browned. Transfer to a bowl. Melt butter in pan. Add onion and garlic to pan. Cook, stirring, for 5 minutes or until softened. Add mushrooms. Cook for 5 minutes or until mushrooms are tender.

3 Add paprika. Cook for 1 minute or until fragrant. Add sour cream and stock. Cook, stirring, over low heat for 2 minutes or until combined. Return beef to pan. Stir to combine. Stir in lemon juice.

4 Divide pasta between bowls. Spoon over stroganoff mixture. Sprinkle with chives. Serve.

NUTRITION: (per serve) 3184kJ; 42.5g fat; 23.5g sat fat; 44.3g protein; 48.3g carbs; 4.5g fibre; 191mg chol; 295mg sodium.

High fibre, lower sodium

FIVE-SPICE BEEF AND HOISIN STIR-FRY

SERVES 4
PREP 15 minutes (plus marinating time)
COOK 20 minutes

⅓ cup hoisin sauce
1 tablespoon light soy sauce
1 tablespoon shao hsing (Chinese rice wine)
¼ teaspoon Chinese five spice
500g beef rump steak, trimmed, thinly sliced
450g packet hokkien noodles
2 tablespoons vegetable oil
1 brown onion, cut into thin wedges
2 garlic cloves, finely chopped
2cm piece fresh ginger, finely grated
1 large red capsicum, cut into 2cm pieces
200g snow peas, trimmed

1 Combine hoisin sauce, soy sauce, shao hsing and five spice in a bowl. Place beef in a glass or ceramic dish. Add half the sauce mixture. Toss to coat. Cover with plastic wrap. Refrigerate for 30 minutes, if time permits. Set remaining sauce aside.

2 Meanwhile, prepare hokkien noodles following packet directions. Drain well and set aside.

3 Heat wok over high heat. Add 2 teaspoons oil. Swirl to coat. Stir-fry a third of the beef for 2 to 3 minutes or until browned. Transfer to a bowl. Cover to keep warm. Repeat with oil and remaining beef in 2 batches.

If necessary, carefully wipe wok clean with paper towel between batches.

4 Add remaining oil to wok over high heat. Swirl to coat. Add onion. Stir-fry for 2 minutes or until softened. Add garlic and ginger. Stir-fry for 1 minute or until fragrant. Add capsicum and snow peas. Stir-fry for 2 to 3 minutes or until tender.

5 Return beef to wok. Add noodles and remaining sauce mixture. Stir-fry for 1 to 2 minutes or until heated through. Serve.

NUTRITION: (per serve) 1856kJ; 16.3g fat; 3.3g sat fat; 30.9g protein; 39.9g carbs; 6.3g fibre; 72mg chol; 947mg sodium.

High fibre, low saturated fat

4 Heat a wok over high heat. Add remaining oil. Swirl to coat. Stir-fry capsicum for 1 minute. Add bok choy. Stir-fry for 1 minute. Add noodles, remaining sauce mixture and 2 tablespoons cold water. Stir-fry for 2 minutes or until heated through. Add meatballs. Toss to combine. Serve.

NUTRITION: (per serve) 2497kJ; 28.7g fat; 7.2g sat fat; 38.3g protein; 43.8g carbs; 6.8g fibre; 116mg chol; 1161mg sodium.

High fibre

CHINESE MEATBALLS WITH HOISIN NOODLES

SERVES 4 **PREP** 20 minutes **COOK** 15 minutes

⅓ cup hoisin sauce
2 tablespoons oyster sauce
1 garlic clove, crushed
2cm fresh ginger, peeled, finely grated
500g beef mince
1 egg
½ cup fresh breadcrumbs
⅓ cup sesame seeds
450g packet hokkien noodles
2 tablespoons vegetable oil
1 medium red capsicum, chopped
1 bunch baby bok choy, roughly chopped

1 Combine sauces, garlic and ginger in a small bowl. Combine mince, egg, breadcrumbs and 2 tablespoons of the sauce mixture in a separate bowl. Place sesame seeds on a plate. Shape level tablespoons of mixture into meatballs and roll in sesame seeds.

2 Place noodles in a medium heatproof bowl. Cover with boiling water. Stand for 3 minutes or until soft. Separate noodles with a fork. Drain.

3 Meanwhile, heat half the oil in a large frying pan over medium heat. Cook meatballs, turning, for 6 to 8 minutes or until cooked through. Transfer meatballs to a plate lined with paper towel.

CHARGRILLED BEEF & CAPSICUM FAJITAS

SERVES 4 **PREP** 15 minutes **COOK** 13 minutes

1 tablespoon garlic pepper seasoning
2 tablespoons olive oil
500g beef rump steak
1 large red capsicum, sliced
1 large yellow capsicum, sliced
1 large green capsicum, sliced
1 red onion, cut into thin wedges
⅓ cup fresh coriander leaves
8 flour tortillas, warmed
Light sour cream and lime wedges, to serve

1 Combine the garlic pepper seasoning and 1 tablespoon oil in a bowl. Rub over steak. Preheat barbecue chargrill and plate on high. Cook steak on chargrill for 3 to 4 minutes each side for medium or until cooked to your liking. Transfer to a plate. Cover loosely with foil. Stand for 5 minutes. Thickly slice.

2 Drizzle remaining oil over barbecue plate. Add capsicum and onion. Cook, tossing, for 5 minutes or until browned and tender.

3 Divide steak, capsicum mixture and coriander leaves between tortillas. Fold tortillas over to enclose filling. Serve with light sour cream and lime wedges.

NUTRITION: (per serve) 2505kJ; 24.6g fat; 8.5g sat fat; 37.1g protein; 53.1g carbs; 4.4g fibre; 92mg chol; 877mg sodium.

SPEEDY MEATBALL & CHICKPEA BRAISE

SERVES 4
PREP 10 minutes
COOK 20 minutes

1½ tablespoons olive oil
1 red onion, cut into thick wedges
2 zucchini, thinly sliced
2 garlic cloves, crushed
1 tablespoon smoked paprika
2 teaspoons ground cumin
410g can tomatoes with paste and herbs (see note)
1½ cups beef stock
400g packet ready-rolled traditional beef meatballs
400g can chickpeas, drained, rinsed
1½ cups couscous
1½ cups boiling water
Chopped fresh flat-leaf parsley leaves, to serve

1 Heat 1 tablespoon oil in a large saucepan over medium-high heat. Add onion and zucchini. Cook, stirring, for 5 minutes or until onion has softened. Add garlic, paprika and cumin. Cook, stirring, for 30 seconds, or until fragrant. Add tomato and stock. Bring to a simmer.

2 Meanwhile, heat remaining oil in a large frying pan over medium-high heat. Add meatballs. Cook, turning, for 2 minutes or until browned.

3 Add meatballs and chickpeas to tomato mixture. Season with salt and pepper. Cover. Bring to a simmer. Reduce heat to medium-low. Cook, stirring occasionally, for 15 minutes or until meatballs are cooked through.

4 Meanwhile, place the couscous in a medium heatproof bowl. Pour over boiling water. Cover. Set aside for 5 minutes or until all the water has been absorbed. Use a fork to separate couscous grains. Sprinkle the meatball mixture with chopped parsley. Serve with couscous.

NUTRITION: (per serve) 2201kJ; 30g fat; 12.4g sat fat; 31g protein; 30.1g carbs; 6.8g fibre; 129mg chol; 865mg sodium.

COOK'S NOTE You could use a can of diced tomatoes and add 1 tablespoon of tomato paste to the mixture.

High fibre

GRILLED STEAK WITH BEETROOT & CHICKPEA SALAD

SERVES 4
PREP 10 minutes
COOK 10 minutes (plus 5 minutes standing time)

4 x 150g beef rump steaks
2 teaspoons olive oil
120g bag four-leaf salad mix
400g can chickpeas, drained, rinsed
450g can baby beets, drained, halved
½ red onion, thinly sliced
½ x 350g jar marinated fetta, reserving
    2 tablespoons marinating oil

1 Brush steaks with olive oil. Season with salt and pepper. Heat a chargrill pan over high heat. Cook steaks for 2 to 3 minutes each side for medium or until cooked to your liking. Rest steaks, loosely covered with foil, for 5 minutes.

2 Combine salad leaves, chickpeas and beets in a large bowl. Top with onion and fetta. Drizzle over marinating oil. Toss to combine.

3 Serve steaks with salad.

NUTRITION: (per serve) 2433kJ; 34.7g fat; 9.5g sat fat; 42.9g protein; 21.6g carbs; 5.5g fibre; 98mg chol; 620mg sodium.

High fibre, high in iron

SPICED BEEF SKEWERS WITH YOGHURT SAUCE

SERVES 4
PREP 30 minutes
COOK 8 minutes
You'll need 8 pre-soaked bamboo skewers
800g beef rump steak, trimmed, cut into 3cm pieces
2 teaspoons ground cumin
2 teaspoons ground coriander
½ teaspoon chilli powder
1½ tablespoons olive oil
2 Lebanese cucumbers
½ cup no-fat plain Greek-style yoghurt
2 garlic cloves, crushed
3 tomatoes, halved, thinly sliced
½ small red onion, thinly sliced
4 naan breads, warmed
Fresh coriander sprigs and lemon wedges, to serve

1 Place beef, cumin, coriander, chilli powder and 1 tablespoon oil in a large bowl. Toss to coat. Thread beef evenly onto 8 skewers.

2 Preheat a barbecue plate or chargrill on medium-high heat. Cook skewers, turning, for 8 minutes for medium or until cooked to your liking.

3 Meanwhile, peel 1 cucumber. Halve both cucumbers lengthways and deseed. Grate peeled cucumber. Thinly slice unpeeled cucumber. Combine grated cucumber, yoghurt and garlic in a small bowl. Combine sliced cucumber, tomato, onion and remaining oil in a large bowl.

4 Place naan, skewers, salad and yoghurt sauce on plates. Serve with coriander sprigs and lemon wedges.

NUTRITION: (per serve) 3150kJ; 24.3g fat; 7.1g sat fat; 57.1g protein; 71.3g carbs; 7.4g fibre; 125mg chol; 1539mg sodium.

High fibre, high in iron

MARSALA VEAL WITH SPINACH & MUSHROOM

SERVES 4

READY in 20 minutes

375g packet fresh fettuccine pasta

4 (500g) veal schnitzels, uncrumbed

2 tablespoons plain flour

2 tablespoons olive oil

50g butter

200g sliced button mushrooms

¼ cup chicken stock

⅓ cup marsala (see note)

½ cup thickened cream

75g baby spinach

1 Cook pasta in a large saucepan of boiling salted water, following packet directions, until tender. Drain. Return to pan. Cover to keep warm.

2 Meanwhile, cut each schnitzel into 3 pieces. Place flour in a shallow dish. Season with salt and pepper. Coat each piece of veal in flour, shaking off excess. Heat oil and half the butter in a large non-stick frying pan over medium-high heat.

3 Cook veal, in batches, for 1 to 2 minutes each side or until light golden. Transfer to a plate. Cover. Set aside.

4 Add mushroom and stock to pan. Cook, stirring, for 2 to 3 minutes or until just tender. Add marsala and cream. Stir to combine. Reduce heat to medium. Return veal to pan with spinach. Stir to combine. Cook for 2 minutes or until spinach has just wilted.

5 Add remaining butter to pasta. Season with salt and pepper. Toss over low heat until butter has melted. Serve pasta with veal mixture.

COOK'S NOTE Marsala is a sweet fortified Italian wine. It is available from most bottle shops.

NUTRITION: (per serve)3082kj; fat 35.5g; sat fat 16g; protein 41.3g; carbs 53.9g; fibre 6g; chol 154mg; sodium 385 mg.

Lower sodium, high fibre

TERIYAKI BEEF & SESAME SOBA NOODLES

SERVES 4　**PREP** 10 minutes　**COOK** 12 minutes
(plus 1 hour refrigeration if time permits)
100g sachet teriyaki beef sauce
600g beef rump steak, trimmed
⅔ x 270g packet dried soba noodles
1½ tablespoons peanut oil
200g snow peas, trimmed, sliced diagonally
2 green onions, thinly sliced
1 tablespoon sesame seeds, lightly toasted

1 Place half the teriyaki sauce in a shallow glass or ceramic dish. Add steak. Turn to coat. Cover. Refrigerate for 1 hour, if time permits.

2 Cook noodles in a saucepan of boiling water, following packet directions, until tender. Drain.

3 Heat 1 tablespoon oil in a large, deep frying pan over medium-high heat (see note). Cook steak for 3 to 4 minutes each side for medium or until cooked to your liking. Transfer steak to a plate. Cover loosely with foil. Set aside for 5 minutes to rest.

4 Meanwhile, heat remaining oil in pan. Add snow peas. Cook for 1 to 2 minutes or until bright green and tender. Add noodles to pan with remaining teriyaki sauce, 1 tablespoon cold water and half the onion. Cook, tossing, for 1 to 2 minutes or until noodles are heated through. Remove from heat. Thinly slice steak. Serve steak on noodles, sprinkle with remaining onion and sesame seeds.

NUTRITION: (per serve) 2080kJ; 15.5g fat; 4.3g sat fat; 39.6g protein; 47.8g carbs; 3g fibre; 91mg chol; 982mg sodium.

COOK'S NOTE You can also cook the beef on a chargrill pan or on the barbecue grill plate.

High in iron, low saturated fat

HERB & GARLIC STEAK OPEN SANDWICHES

SERVES 4　**PREP** 10 minutes　**COOK** 10 minutes
2 tablespoons olive oil
1 tablespoon Italian herbs paste (see notes)
1 tablespoon chunky garlic paste
4 (450g) beef silverside sandwich steaks
8 slices traditional bruschettina bread (see notes)
Olive oil cooking spray
8 small butter lettuce leaves
2 vine-ripened tomatoes, sliced
200g tub beetroot dip

1 Combine oil, and herb and garlic pastes in a shallow glass or ceramic dish. Season with salt and pepper. Add steaks. Turn to coat. Heat a large non-stick frying pan over medium-high heat. Cook steak, in batches, for 2 minutes each side for medium or until cooked to your liking. Transfer to a plate. Cover to keep warm.

2 Preheat grill on high. Spray 1 side of each slice of bread with oil. Place on a baking tray, oil-side up. Grill bread for 2 minutes or until toasted. Place 2 slices of toast, overlapping, onto each plate. Top with lettuce, tomato and steaks. Serve with a dollop of beetroot dip.

COOK'S NOTES Italian herbs paste is in the fresh herb section of supermarkets. Bruschettina is in the bakery section.

NUTRITION: (per serve) 2102kj; fat 19.3g; sat fat 4.3g; protein 36.9g; carbs 42.1g; fibre 4.1g; chol 41mg; sodium 1054 mg.

LAMB

LEBANESE-SPICED LAMB SKEWERS WITH ROASTED CAULIFLOWER SALAD

SERVES 4

PREP 25 minutes

COOK 20 minutes

You'll need 8 pre-soaked bamboo skewers

750g cauliflower, cut into florets

1 tablespoon olive oil

3 garlic cloves

1 tablespoon sesame seeds

2 teaspoons sumac

½ teaspoon ground allspice

2 tablespoons olive oil

600g diced lamb

250g baby green beans

1 small red onion, thinly sliced

2 tablespoons lemon juice

lemon wedges, to serve

Garlic yoghurt dip

¾ cup plain Greek-style yoghurt

2 garlic cloves, crushed

1 tablespoon lemon juice

½ teaspoon sumac

1 Preheat oven to 200°C/180°C fan-forced. Line 2 large baking trays with baking paper. Place cauliflower in a bowl. Add oil and 1 clove of garlic, crushed. Season with salt and pepper. Toss to coat. Arrange cauliflower mixture, in a single layer, on prepared trays. Roast for 20 minutes or until cauliflower is golden and tender. Keep cauliflower warm.

2 Meanwhile, combine sesame seeds, sumac and allspice in a small bowl. Combine half the oil and remaining garlic in a large bowl. Add lamb. Toss to coat in oil mixture. Thread lamb onto skewers. Sprinkle all over with sesame seed mixture.

3 Make Garlic yoghurt dip. Combine yoghurt, garlic, lemon juice and sumac in a small jug. Season with salt and pepper.

4 Heat a barbecue plate or chargrill on medium-high heat. Cook skewers in batches, turning, for 6 to 8 minutes for medium or until cooked to your liking.

5 Meanwhile, cook beans in a medium saucepan of boiling water for 3 to 4 minutes or until just tender. Drain. Rinse under cold water. Place beans in a medium bowl. Add cauliflower and onion. Place lemon juice in a small bowl with remaining oil and garlic. Whisk until combined. Season with salt and pepper. Add lemon juice mixture to salad. Toss gently to combine.

6 Serve skewers with salad, garlic yoghurt dip and lemon wedges.

NUTRITION: (per serve) 1932kJ; 27.8g fat; 7.4g sat fat; 40.8g protein; 10g carbs; 5.3g fibre; 126mg chol; 23mg sodium.

High in iron, high in fibre

SESAME LAMB PATTIES WITH CHICKPEA SALAD

SERVES 4

PREP 30 minutes

COOK 6 minutes

1 teaspoon cumin seeds

2 teaspoons ground coriander

1 cup fresh breadcrumbs

600g lamb mince

2 garlic cloves, crushed

3 green onions, thinly sliced

½ cup chopped fresh mint leaves

⅓ cup sesame seeds

2 tablespoons olive oil

½ cup plain Greek-style yoghurt

2 tablespoons lemon juice

1½ tablespoons tahini

75g baby spinach

4 radishes, trimmed, thinly sliced

400g can chickpeas, drained, rinsed

Lemon wedges, to serve

1 Combine cumin, coriander, breadcrumbs, mince, garlic, onion and half the mint in a bowl. Season with salt and pepper. Divide into 8 portions, then roll into balls. Flatten slightly. Place patties on a plate. Place sesame seeds on a separate plate. Coat patties in seeds on both sides. Return to plate.

2 Heat a barbecue hotplate on medium-high heat. Drizzle with half the oil. Cook patties for 2 to 3 minutes each side or until golden and cooked through.

3 Combine yoghurt, lemon juice and tahini in a small bowl. Toss spinach, radish, chickpeas and remaining mint and oil in a medium bowl. Season with salt and pepper.

4 Serve lamb patties with chickpea salad, tahini yoghurt and lemon wedges.

NUTRITION: (per serve) 2526kJ; 35.7g fat; 8.9g sat fat; 44g protein; 23.2g carbs; 7.9g fibre; 96mg chol; 395mg sodium.

High fibre, high in iron, lower sodium

MONGOLIAN LAMB CHOPS WITH RICE SALAD

SERVES 4

PREP 15 minutes (plus 1 hour marinating)

COOK 10 minutes

¼ cup soy sauce

2 tablespoons black bean sauce

1 tablespoon brown sugar

¼ cup rice vinegar

2 garlic cloves, crushed

8 x 100g lamb chump chops

2 teaspoons cornflour

3 cups cooked jasmine rice (see note)

100g snow peas, trimmed, thinly sliced

1½ cups bean sprouts

3 green onions, thinly sliced

1 small red capsicum, thinly sliced

1 tablespoon sesame oil

Extra sliced green onions, to serve

1 Combine sauces, sugar, half the vinegar and half the garlic in a large shallow glass or ceramic dish. Add lamb. Turn to coat. Refrigerate for 1 hour.

2 Heat a chargrill or barbecue plate on medium-high heat. Drain lamb, reserving marinade. Cook lamb for 3 to 4 minutes each side or until cooked to your liking. Transfer to a plate. Cover loosely with foil. Set aside for 5 minutes.

3 Meanwhile, place reserved marinade in a small saucepan over medium heat. Bring to the boil. Blend cornflour in a small jug with 2 teaspoons cold water. Stir cornflour mixture into marinade. Cook, stirring, until sauce thickens slightly. Remove from heat. Cover.

4 Combine rice, snow peas, sprouts, onion and capsicum in a medium bowl. Place oil, remaining vinegar and remaining garlic in a small bowl. Whisk until well combined. Season with salt and pepper. Add dressing to salad. Toss gently to combine. Drizzle lamb with sauce. Sprinkle with extra green onions. Serve with rice salad.

NUTRITION: (per serve) 2317kJ; 20.8g fat; 6.9g sat fat; 37.7g protein; 52.3g carbs; 3.4g fibre; 92mg chol; 1578mg sodium.

COOK'S NOTE You will need to cook 1 cup jasmine rice for this recipe. Alternatively, use microwave express rice.

3 Meanwhile, make Ranch dressing Place mayonnaise, buttermilk, vinegar, garlic, chives and paprika in a small screw-top jar. Shake well to combine. Season. Drizzle lettuce with Ranch dressing. Serve with skewers.

NUTRITION: (per serve) 2199kJ; 34.2g fat; 5.8g sat fat; 37g protein; 17g carbs; 4.2g fibre; 142mg chol; 200mg sodium.

High in iron, lower sodium, low saturated fat

FAST-COOKED LAMB & DATE TAGINE

SERVES 4   **PREP** 15 minutes   **COOK** 30 minutes
2 tablespoons olive oil
500g lamb leg steaks, thinly sliced
1 medium red onion, cut into wedges
2 teaspoons paprika
1 teaspoon ground cumin
2 tablespoons honey
400g orange sweet potato, peeled, cut into 2cm cubes
1 cinnamon stick
1 cup beef stock
6 fresh dates, pitted, halved
Couscous, fresh coriander leaves, toasted slivered almonds and paprika, extra, to serve

1 Heat 1 tablespoon oil in a large saucepan over medium-high heat. Add lamb. Cook, in 2 batches, for 2 minutes or until browned all over. Transfer to a plate.

2 Heat remaining oil in pan. Add onion. Cook for 3 minutes or until softened. Add paprika, cumin and honey. Cook, stirring, for 1 minute or until fragrant. Add sweet potato. Cook, stirring, for 1 minute or until coated. Add cinnamon stick and beef stock. Bring to the boil. Reduce heat to low. Simmer, covered, for 10 minutes or until sauce is slightly thickened. Add dates. Simmer for 5 minutes or until sweet potato is cooked through and tender.

3 Add lamb to sweet potato. Cook, stirring occasionally for 3 minutes or until lamb is cooked to your liking. Spoon couscous into bowls. Top with lamb mixture. Sprinkle with coriander, almonds and paprika. Serve.

NUTRITION: (per serve) 2994kj; fat 24.7g; sat fat 6.1g; protein 48.4g; carbs 73.9g; fibre 5g; chol 104mg; sodium 375 mg.

Healthy, lower sodium, low saturated fat

LAMB, SWEET POTATO & ROSEMARY SKEWERS

SERVES 4   **PREP** 30 minutes   **COOK** 15 minutes
You'll need 8 pre-soaked bamboo skewers
1 (400g) sweet potato, cut into 3cm pieces
2 tablespoons olive oil
2 garlic cloves, crushed
2 tablespoons chopped fresh rosemary leaves
600g diced lamb
1 large red onion, cut into thin wedges
1 small iceberg lettuce, cored, cut into 8 wedges
Ranch dressing
⅓ cup whole-egg mayonnaise
2 tablespoons buttermilk
1 tablespoon white wine vinegar
1 garlic clove, crushed
1 tablespoon finely chopped fresh chives
¼ teaspoon sweet paprika

1 Cook sweet potato in a saucepan of boiling water for 4 to 5 minutes or until almost tender. Drain. Cool. Combine oil, garlic and rosemary in a large bowl. Add lamb. Toss to coat in oil mixture.

2 Thread lamb, potato and onion alternately onto skewers. Heat a barbecue plate or chargrill on medium-high heat. Cook skewers, turning, for 6 to 8 minutes for medium or until cooked to your liking.

Toss gently to combine. Drizzle sweet potato with harissa yoghurt. Serve lamb chops with sweet potato, salad and lemon wedges.

NUTRITION: (per serve) 2457kJ; 38.9g fat; 10.9g sat fat; 33.3g protein; 24.6g carbs; 4.8g fibre; 92mg chol; 195mg sodium.

COOK'S NOTE Harissa paste is a spicy paste used in North African cookery. Find in large supermarkets.

high in iron, lower sodium

LAMB STEAKS WITH ORANGE, BEETROOT & AVOCADO SALAD

SERVES 4   **PREP** 17 minutes   **COOK** 8 minutes

4 (600g) lean lamb leg steaks
1 orange
¼ cup olive oil
2 teaspoons wholegrain mustard
50g mixed salad leaves
450g can baby beetroot, drained, cut into wedges
¼ cup walnut pieces
1 medium avocado, sliced
50g fetta cheese, crumbled

1 Heat a greased barbecue plate or chargrill on medium heat. Cook steaks for 4 minutes each side for medium, or until cooked to your liking. Transfer to a plate. Cover with foil. Rest for 5 minutes.

2 Peel and segment orange (see note), reserving 2 tablespoons juice. Combine reserved orange juice, oil and mustard in a screw-top jar. Season with salt and pepper. Secure lid. Shake to combine.

3 Combine orange segments, salad leaves, beetroot, walnuts and avocado in a bowl. Drizzle over half the dressing. Gently toss to combine. Place steaks on plates. Serve with salad mixture and crumble over fetta. Drizzle with remaining dressing. Serve.

NUTRITION: (per serve) 2486kj; fat 42.9g; sat fat 9.7g; protein 38.4g; carbs 12.4g; fibre 4.1g; chol 104mg; sodium 565 mg.

COOK'S NOTE To segment orange, remove peel and pith. Cut either side of the membrane to release segments. Squeeze membrane over a bowl to catch the juice.

LAMB CHOPS WITH HARISSA YOGHURT

SERVES 4   **PREP** 15 minutes   **COOK** 10 minutes

500g sweet potato, washed
2 tablespoons olive oil
4 (200g each) lamb forequarter chops
¾ cup light Greek-style yoghurt
2 teaspoons harissa paste (see note)
2 tablespoons chopped fresh coriander leaves
2 witlof, leaves separated
1 cup fresh flat-leaf parsley leaves
½ cup fresh coriander leaves
1 tablespoon lemon juice
Lemon wedges, to serve

1 Using a fork, pierce sweet potato all over. Place on a microwave-safe plate. Microwave on HIGH (100%) for 4 minutes or until tender. Quarter sweet potato lengthways. Brush with half the oil.

2 Heat a greased barbecue plate or chargrill on medium-high. Cook lamb for 3 to 4 minutes each side for medium or until cooked to your liking. Cook sweet potato for 2 to 3 minutes each side or until crisp.

3 Place yoghurt, harissa paste and chopped coriander in a small bowl. Stir to combine. Combine witlof, parsley leaves and coriander leaves in a medium bowl. Drizzle with lemon juice and remaining oil.

LAMB & LEMONY HUMMUS FLATBREADS

SERVES 4

PREP 15 minutes

COOK 10 minutes (plus 5 minutes standing)

400g can chickpeas, drained, rinsed

1 tablespoon tahini (see box)

⅓ cup lemon zest (see note)

⅔ cup lemon juice

⅓ cup extra virgin olive oil

2 garlic cloves, crushed

1 tablespoon finely chopped

fresh flat-leaf parsley

500g lamb rump steaks

4 small wholemeal pita breads

¼ cup pistachio kernels, finely chopped

½ cup pitted green olives, chopped

Extra ½ cup fresh flat-leaf parsley leaves

Mixed salad leaves, to serve

1 Place chickpeas, tahini, half the lemon zest, half the lemon juice and half the oil in a food processor. Process until smooth and combined, scraping down sides of processor occasionally. Season with salt and pepper. Spoon into a bowl. Set aside.

2 Heat a large chargrill pan over medium-high heat. Combine garlic, finely chopped parsley and remaining oil in bowl. Season with salt and pepper. Drizzle half the oil mixture on both sides of the lamb. Cook for 3 minutes each side for medium or until cooked to your liking. Cover loosely with foil. Set aside for 5 minutes to rest. Thinly slice.

3 Brush remaining oil mixture over both sides of breads. Chargrill for 1 minute each side or until golden and crisp. Spread warm breads with three-quarters of the hummus. Top with lamb, sprinkle with remaining lemon rind and juice. Top with pistachios, olives and extra parsley. Serve with mixed salad leaves and remaining hummus.

NUTRITION: (per serve) 2957kJ; 31.8g fat; 12.3g sat fat; 41.8g protein; 60.2g carbs; 5.8g fibre; 87mg chol; 1724mg sodium.

COOK'S NOTE You will need to zest the skin of 2 large lemons.

High fibre, low saturated fat

GRILLED LAMB STEAKS WITH LEMON PARSLEY & CHILLI DRESSING

SERVES 4   **PREP** 15 minutes   **COOK** 22 minutes

700g chat potatoes, halved
4 (600g) corn cobs, trimmed, each cut into 3 pieces
200g green beans, trimmed, sliced
1 lemon
1 long red chilli, finely chopped
1 long green chilli, finely chopped
⅓ cup extra virgin olive oil
4 lamb leg steaks
½ cup finely chopped fresh flat-leaf parsley leaves

1 Place potato in a large saucepan of cold, salted water. Bring to the boil. Boil for 5 minutes. Add corn. Boil for 3 minutes. Add beans. Boil for a further 4 minutes or until all vegetables are just tender. Drain. Return to pan. Cover to keep warm.

2 Meanwhile, finely grate lemon rind (you need 2 teaspoons). Halve lemon. Remove skin and pith from 1 half and dice the flesh. Juice remaining lemon half (you'll need 1 tablespoon juice). Combine lemon rind, diced lemon, lemon juice, chilli and 3½ tablespoons oil in a jar. Season with salt and pepper. Secure lid. Shake to combine. Set aside.

3 Preheat a chargrill on medium-high. Brush steaks with remaining oil. Season with salt and pepper. Chargrill steaks for 4 to 5 minutes each side, for medium, or until cooked to your liking. Stir parsley through chilli dressing. Serve lamb and vegetables drizzled with chilli dressing.

NUTRITION: (per serve) 3035kJ; 38.4g fat; 10g sat fat; 40.2g protein; 49.9g carbs; 9.7g fibre; 105mg chol; 281mg sodium.

High fibre, gluten free, lower sodium

INDIAN LAMB BAKE

SERVES 4   **PREP** 8 minutes   **COOK** 37 minutes

1 tablespoon olive oil
8 (100g each) lamb chump chops
540g jar rogan josh simmer sauce
500g bag frozen carrots, cauliflower and broccoli
Olive oil cooking spray
4 plain naan breads
⅓ cup fresh coriander leaves
Plain Greek-style yoghurt and mango chutney, to serve

1 Preheat oven to 200°C/180°C fan-forced. Heat oil in a large non-stick frying pan over medium-high heat. Add lamb. Cook for 2 minutes each side or until browned. Remove from heat.

2 Grease a large roasting pan. Add rogan josh sauce and frozen vegetables. Toss to combine. Add lamb. Turn to coat in sauce. Spray with oil. Bake for 20 to 25 minutes or until lamb is cooked and vegetables are tender.

3 Sprinkle naan bread with 1 teaspoon cold water. Wrap in foil. Bake in oven for 6 to 8 minutes. Add naan to oven in the last 10 minutes of the lamb's cooking time.

4 Sprinkle lamb with coriander leaves. Serve with warm naan bread, yoghurt and mango chutney.

NUTRITION: (per serve) 3402kj; fat 33.9g; sat fat 13.1g; protein 42.3g; carbs 80.2g; fibre 8.5g; chol 104mg; sodium 1752 mg.

High fibre

LAMB WITH FETTA & OLIVE STUFFED PEPPERS

SERVES 4

PREP 15 minutes

COOK 25 minutes

4 red bullhorn peppers, halved lengthways

100g fetta, crumbled

8 cherry tomatoes, thickly sliced

¼ cup pitted kalamata olives, halved

2 garlic cloves, finely chopped

2 tablespoons olive oil

500g lamb leg steaks

2 tablespoons finely grated lemon rind

Mixed salad leaves, lemon cheeks and ¼ cup small fresh basil leaves, to serve

1 Preheat oven to 200°C/180°C fan-forced. Line a baking tray with baking paper. Remove seeds and membranes from peppers. Place peppers, cut-side up, on prepared tray. Sprinkle with ⅔ of the fetta. Top with tomato, olives and garlic. Sprinkle with remaining fetta. Drizzle with half the oil. Bake for 25 minutes or until peppers are tender.

2 Meanwhile, drizzle steaks with remaining oil. Sprinkle both sides with lemon rind. Season with salt and pepper. Heat a barbecue hotplate or chargrill on medium-high heat. Cook steaks for 2 to 3 minutes each side, for medium, or until browned and cooked to your liking.

3 Serve steaks with peppers, salad leaves and lemon wedges. Sprinkle with basil.

NUTRITION: (per serve) 1862kJ; 26.5g fat; 9.6g sat fat; 43.8g protein; 6.6g carbs; 2.8g fibre; 120mg chol; 475mg sodium.

Lower sodium

MONGOLIAN LAMB WITH NOODLES

SERVES 4
PREP 15 minutes
COOK 10 minutes

120g sachet Mongolian lamb sauce
700g lamb leg steaks
440g packet shelf-fresh hokkien noodles
1 tablespoon peanut oil
1 red onion, cut into thick wedges
2 garlic cloves, thinly sliced
1 teaspoon sesame seeds
150g snow peas, trimmed, halved
Sliced long red chilli (optional), to serve

1 Combine half the Mongolian sauce with 1 tablespoon cold water in a small bowl. Heat a chargrill pan over medium-high heat. Cook lamb, brushing with sauce mixture, for 3 minutes each side for medium or until cooked to your liking. Transfer to a plate. Cover loosely with foil. Rest for 5 minutes. Thickly slice.

2 Meanwhile, place noodles in a heatproof bowl. Cover with boiling water. Stand for 1 minute. Separate noodles with a fork. Drain. Set aside.

3 Heat a wok over high heat. Add oil. Swirl to coat. Add onion. Stir-fry for 2 minutes or until starting to soften. Add garlic, sesame seeds and snow peas. Stir-fry for 2 minutes or until peas are bright green. Add noodles, remaining Mongolian sauce and 2 tablespoons cold water. Stir-fry for 1 minute or until heated through.

4 Serve lamb on noodles and top with chilli, if using.

NUTRITION: (per serve) 1988kJ; 17.1g fat; 6.3g sat fat; 43.4g protein; 34.7g carbs; 3.4g fibre; 119mg chol; 560mg sodium.

High fibre

LAMB KEBABS WITH CAULIFLOWER MASH & PARSLEY SAUCE

SERVES 4
PREP 20 minutes
COOK 15 minutes

You'll need 12 small pre-soaked bamboo skewers

700g cauliflower, cut into florets
2 large potatoes, peeled, chopped
½ cup milk
30g butter, melted
750g diced lamb
2 tablespoons Greek seasoning
1 tablespoon extra virgin olive oil
240g cherry truss tomatoes

Parsley sauce
3 cups roughly chopped fresh flat-leaf parsley leaves
2 tablespoons lemon juice
2 tablespoons extra virgin olive oil
1 garlic clove, crushed
2 teaspoons drained capers

1 Cook cauliflower and potato in saucepan of boiling salted water for 15 minutes or until tender. Drain. Return to pan over low heat. Toss for 1 minute or until excess liquid has evaporated. Remove from heat. Add milk and butter. Mash. Season with salt and pepper. Cover to keep warm.

2 Meanwhile, combine lamb, seasoning and oil in a bowl. Thread lamb onto skewers.

3 Heat a chargrill pan over medium heat. Cook kebabs, in batches, turning for 5 to 6 minutes, for medium or until cooked to your liking. Transfer to a large plate. Cover loosely with foil. Rest for 5 minutes.

4 Place cherry tomatoes in chargrill pan. Cook, turning occasionally, for 2 minutes or until starting to soften.

5 Make Parsley sauce Combine all ingredients in a bowl. Season with salt and pepper.

6 Serve mash, kebabs and tomatoes drizzled with parsley sauce.

NUTRITION: (per serve) 2453kJ; 31.4g fat; 10g sat fat; 50.2g protein; 23.2g carbs; 7.5g fibre; 170mg chol; 1525mg sodium.

High fibre, high in iron

PORK

WARM PORK & PEAR SALAD

SERVES 4
PREP 15 minutes
COOK 8 minutes (plus 5 minutes standing time)
500g pork fillet
1½ tablespoons extra virgin olive oil
2 beurre bosc pears, cored, thinly sliced
½ x 180g bag baby salad leaf mix with beetroot
½ cup walnuts, toasted, roughly chopped
100g mild blue cheese, crumbled
¼ cup red wine vinegar

1 Drizzle pork with 2 teaspoons olive oil. Season with salt and pepper. Heat a chargrill pan over medium-high heat. Cook pork, turning, for 7 to 8 minutes or until browned all over and just cooked through. Transfer to a plate. Cover. Stand for 5 minutes.

2 Slice pork thickly.

3 Place pork, pear, salad mix, walnuts and blue cheese in a bowl. Place vinegar and remaining oil in a screw-top jar. Season with salt and pepper. Secure lid. Shake to combine. Drizzle dressing over salad. Toss gently to combine. Serve.

NUTRITION: (per serve) 1843kJ; 27.1g fat; 7.7g sat fat; 35g protein; 12.8g carbs; 3.6g fibre; 144mg chol; 415mg sodium.

SWEET & SOUR PORK

SERVES 4
PREP 20 minutes
COOK 15 minutes
1 egg
2 tablespoons cornflour
600g pork fillet, thinly sliced
440g can pineapple pieces in natural juice
½ cup tomato sauce
¼ cup soy sauce
2 tablespoons white vinegar
2 tablespoons peanut oil
1 large brown onion, halved, thinly sliced
2 green onions, cut into 2.5cm lengths
2 garlic cloves, crushed
½ red capsicum, chopped
½ green capsicum, chopped
Steamed jasmine rice, to serve

1 Whisk egg and half the cornflour together in a bowl. Add pork. Stir to combine.

2 Drain pineapple, reserving 2 tablespoons of juice. Place remaining cornflour in a bowl. Add reserved juice. Stir until smooth. Add tomato sauce, soy sauce and vinegar. Stir to combine.

3 Heat a wok over medium-high heat until hot. Add 1 tablespoon oil. Swirl to coat. Stir-fry pork, in batches, for 1 to 2 minutes or until browned. Transfer to a bowl.

4 Add remaining oil to wok. Swirl to coat. Add onions and garlic. Stir-fry for 2 minutes or until softened. Add capsicum. Stir-fry for 3 to 4 minutes or until capsicum starts to soften.

5 Return pork and any juices to wok. Add sauce mixture and pineapple. Stir-fry for 2 to 3 minutes or until sauce boils and thickens. Serve with steamed rice.

NUTRITION: (per serve) 2689kJ; 14.6g fat; 3.4g sat fat; 43.5g protein; 79.6g carbs; 4g fibre; 189mg chol; 1435mg sodium.

Low saturated fat

PORK TONKATSU WITH COLESLAW

SERVES 4
PREP 15 minutes
COOK 15 minutes

2 tablespoons Japanese-style mayonnaise
1 tablespoon lemon juice
5 cups (250g) finely shredded Chinese cabbage (wombok)
2 carrots, cut into ribbons (see note)
3 green onions, trimmed, thinly sliced diagonally
400g pork loin steaks
¼ cup plain flour
1 egg
1 cup panko breadcrumbs
⅓ cup rice bran oil
Steamed white rice, hot English mustard, soy sauce and extra mayonnaise, to serve

1 Place mayonnaise and lemon juice in a large bowl. Season with salt and pepper. Whisk with a fork until combined. Add cabbage, carrot and green onion. Toss to coat.

2 Place 1 steak between 2 sheets of baking paper. Using a rolling pin, pound until almost doubled in area. Repeat with remaining steaks. Place flour on a large plate. Season with salt and pepper. Whisk egg and 2 teaspoons cold water together in a shallow bowl. Place breadcrumbs on a large plate. Coat 1 steak in flour, shaking off excess. Dip in egg mixture. Coat in breadcrumbs. Place on a large plate. Repeat with remaining ingredients.

3 Heat oil in a frying pan over medium-high heat. Cook pork, in 2 batches, for 3 minutes each side, or until golden and just cooked. Transfer to a plate lined with paper towel.

4 Cut each steak into 2cm slices and arrange on plates. Serve with coleslaw, rice, mustard, soy sauce and extra mayonnaise.

NUTRITION: (per serve) 3154kJ; 36.2g fat; 6.6g sat fat; 37.3g protein; 60.5g carbs; 5g fibre; 139mg chol; 1565mg sodium.

COOK'S NOTE Use a vegetable peeler to cut carrots into ribbons.

CHEESY HAM & ASPARAGUS CREPES

SERVES 4
PREP 5 minutes
COOK 15 minutes

2 bunches asparagus, trimmed
400g packet frozen French-style crepes
4 large slices leg ham, halved
1 cup grated tasty cheese
½ cup thickened cream
¼ cup grated parmesan
Garden salad, to serve

1 Cook asparagus in a large saucepan of boiling salted water for 3 minutes until just tender. Drain.

2 Preheat grill on high. Top each crepe with 1 piece of ham, 2 asparagus spears and 1 tablespoon tasty cheese. Roll up to enclose filling. Place crepes in a 22cm x 35cm ovenproof baking dish. Top with any remaining asparagus spears. Pour over cream. Sprinkle with parmesan and remaining tasty cheese. Season with pepper. Grill for 10 minutes or until cheese has melted and cream is bubbling. Serve immediately with salad.

NUTRITION: (per serve) 2216kJ; 32g fat; 17.9g sat fat; 23.5g protein; 36.6g carbs; 2.3g fibre; 94mg chol; 1215mg sodium.

PORK WITH APPLE & WATERCRESS SALAD

SERVES 4

PREP 10 minutes

COOK 20 minutes

½ cup whole-berry cranberry sauce

1½ tablespoons French dressing

500g piece pork fillet, trimmed (see notes)

2 large pink lady apples, cored, thinly sliced (see notes)

Olive oil cooking spray

1 bunch (350g) watercress, trimmed

½ cup walnut pieces, toasted

1 Place cranberry sauce in a heatproof, microwave-safe bowl. Microwave on HIGH (100%) for 1 minute or until melted. Transfer 2 tablespoons sauce to a small bowl. Add dressing. Stir to combine. Set aside. Place pork on a plate. Brush with half the remaining sauce. Place apples in a bowl. Add remaining sauce. Toss to coat.

2 Preheat barbecue (with hood) hot plate on high heat. Spray pork lightly with oil. Season well with salt and pepper. Reduce barbecue heat to medium-high. Cook pork for 3 minutes each side. Reduce heat to low. Close barbecue hood. Cook pork for a further 8 minutes or until cooked through. Transfer to a plate. Cover loosely with foil. Set aside for 10 minutes to rest.

3 Increase barbecue hot plate to medium-high heat. Cook apple slices, turning, for 2 to 3 minutes or until charred and tender. Place watercress, apple, walnuts and dressing in a bowl. Toss to combine. Serve salad with pork.

NUTRITION: (per serve) 1563kJ; 13.3g fat; 1.4g sat fat; 33.4g protein; 27.9g carbs; 6.2g fibre; 59mg chol; 305mg sodium.

COOK'S NOTES
You can use 4 pork scotch fillet steaks or pork loin medallions for the fillet. Make the most of summer fruit and replace apples with peaches.

Low fat, lower GI, heart friendly

FENNEL & THYME PORK WITH ASPARAGUS & ROCKET SALAD

SERVES 4
PREP 20 minutes
COOK 15 minutes

600g baby chat potatoes, halved
2 teaspoons fennel seeds, crushed (see notes)
2 teaspoons finely chopped fresh thyme
2 teaspoons finely chopped fresh rosemary
½ teaspoon sea salt flakes
4 pork cutlets, trimmed
2 tablespoons olive oil
2 tablespoons lemon juice
1 bunch asparagus, cut into ribbons (see notes)
60g baby rocket
½ x 400g can cannellini beans, drained, rinsed
¼ cup shaved parmesan
Lemon wedges, to serve

1 Cook potatoes in a saucepan of boiling water for 15 minutes or until just tender. Drain. Return to pan. Cover to keep warm.

2 Meanwhile, combine fennel seeds, thyme, rosemary and salt in a bowl. Drizzle pork with half the oil. Sprinkle both sides with thyme mixture. Heat a barbecue hotplate or chargrill on medium-high heat. Cook pork for 3 to 4 minutes each side or until browned and cooked through. Transfer to a plate. Cover with foil. Set aside to rest.

3 Place lemon juice and remaining oil in a bowl. Whisk to combine. Add asparagus, rocket, cannellini beans and parmesan. Season with salt and pepper. Toss to combine. Serve pork with potatoes, salad and lemon wedges.

NUTRITION: (per serve) 1810kJ; 14.7g fat; 3.3g sat fat; 44.5g protein; 26.2g carbs; 7.2g fibre; 75mg chol; 445mg sodium.

COOK'S NOTES
Place fennel seeds in a snap-lock bag, seal and pound with a rolling pin. Use a vegetable peeler to make asparagus ribbons.

Lower sodium, high fibre, low GI

PORK MILANESE WITH CREAMY PASTA

SERVES 4

PREP 20 minutes

COOK 15 minutes

¼ cup plain flour

2 eggs, lightly beaten

1 cup grated four cheese blend

2½ cups fresh breadcrumbs

4 x 125g pork leg schnitzels, uncrumbed, halved crossways

2 cups mini penne rigate

1 garlic clove, crushed

300ml pure cream

2 green onions, thinly sliced

2 tablespoons finely chopped fresh chives

2 tablespoons olive oil

300g green beans, trimmed

1 Place flour on a plate. Pour egg into a shallow bowl. Finely chop ⅓ cup cheese. Combine breadcrumbs and chopped cheese on a plate. Coat 1 piece pork in flour, shaking off excess. Dip in egg. Coat in breadcrumb mixture. Place on a plate. Repeat with remaining pork, flour, egg and breadcrumb.

2 Place penne, garlic, cream and 2 cups cold water in a saucepan over medium-high heat. Bring to the boil. Reduce heat to medium-low. Simmer, uncovered, for 8 to 10 minutes or until pasta is tender and sauce has thickened. Remove from heat. Stir in ⅔ of the onion and chives and remaining cheese. Season.

3 Meanwhile, heat oil in a large frying pan over medium-high heat. Cook pork, in batches, for 2 to 3 minutes on each side or until golden and cooked through. Cook beans in a saucepan of boiling water for 1 to 2 minutes or until just tender. Drain. Serve with pasta and beans and sprinkled with remaining onion and chives.

NUTRITION: (per serve) 4224kj; fat 48.7g; sat fat 24.2g; protein 52.6g; carbs 85.7g; fibre 6.5g; chol 237mg; sodium 497 mg.

High fibre, lower sodium

BARBECUED CORN & CHORIZO SALAD

SERVES 4

PREP 15 minutes

COOK 20 minutes

4 corn cobs, husks and silk removed

2 (125g each) chorizo sausages, sliced

1 medium capsicum, finely chopped

1 medium avocado, chopped

100g baby roma tomatoes, halved

½ cup fresh coriander leaves, chopped

2 tablespoons lime juice

1 Place corn on a microwave-safe plate. Cover with plastic wrap. Microwave on HIGH (100%) for 4 minutes.

2 Heat barbecue plate on medium heat. Cook corn, turning, for 8 to 10 minutes or until browned. Transfer to a plate. Set aside for 2 minutes to cool slightly. Add chorizo to barbecue plate. Cook, turning, for 2 minutes or until browned all over. Remove.

3 When corn is cool enough to handle, use a sharp knife to slice kernels from cob. Place corn kernels, chorizo, capsicum, avocado, tomato, coriander and lime juice in a bowl. Season with salt and pepper. Toss to combine. Serve.

NUTRITION: (per serve) 1953kJ; 33.9g fat; 11.3g sat fat; 18.7g protein; 20.1g carbs; 4.1g fibre; 30mg chol; 955mg sodium.

High fibre

PORK WITH PEAR & FENNEL SALAD & WALNUT CRUMBLE

SERVES 4

PREP 20 minutes

COOK 10 minutes

1 tablespoon olive oil

4 x 150g each pork loin medallions

⅓ cup walnuts, chopped

2 teaspoons finely grated lemon rind

½ cup finely grated parmesan

2 corella pears, quartered, cored, sliced

2 fennel bulbs, trimmed, thinly sliced, fronds reserved

1 tablespoon lemon juice

1 Heat 2 teaspoons oil in a frying pan over medium-high heat. Add pork. Cook for 2 to 3 minutes each side or until cooked through. Transfer to a plate. Cover loosely with foil. Rest for 5 minutes.

2 Meanwhile, wipe pan clean. Place over medium heat. Add walnuts and lemon rind. Cook, stirring occasionally, for 3 to 4 minutes or until walnuts are toasted. Add parmesan. Cook, stirring, for 1 to 2 minutes or until parmesan is melted and mixture is well combined.

3 Place pear and fennel in a bowl. Add lemon juice, fronds and remaining oil. Season with salt and pepper. Toss to combine. Divide fennel mixture and pork between plates. Sprinkle with walnut crumble. Serve.

NUTRITION: (per serve) 2001kJ; 30g fat; 9.2g sat fat; 34.7g protein; 15.5g carbs; 5.8g fibre; 145mg chol; 320mg sodium.

Lower sodium, high fibre

CHORIZO & BROAD BEAN SALAD

SERVES 4   **PREP** 10 minutes   **COOK** 10 minutes
⅓ cup extra virgin olive oil
4 garlic cloves, crushed
1 loaf ciabatta, sliced diagonally into 8 pieces
3 (125g each) chorizo sausages, sliced
2 red onions, cut into thin wedges
2 tablespoons red wine vinegar
500g packet frozen broad beans, thawed, peeled
½ cup fresh mint leaves
½ cup fresh flat-leaf parsley leaves

1 Combine ¼ cup oil and half the garlic in a bowl. Brush both sides of bread slices with oil mixture. Heat a barbecue chargrill and plate on medium heat. Add bread to barbecue chargrill. Cook for 1 to 2 minutes each side or until golden and beginning to char. Transfer to a platter.

2 Place chorizo, onion and remaining garlic in a bowl. Add remaining oil. Toss to coat. Add chorizo mixture to barbecue plate. Cook, gently tossing, for 4 to 6 minutes or until chorizo is crisp and onion is tender. Transfer to a heatproof bowl. Add vinegar, broad beans, mint and parsley. Season with pepper. Toss to combine.

3 Spoon chorizo mixture over bread. Serve.

NUTRITION: (per serve) 3581kJ; 51.1g fat; 16.3g sat fat; 38.1g protein; 57.7g carbs; 11.7g fibre; 45mg chol; 1885mg sodium.

High fibre

FIVE-SPICE PORK & GREENS

SERVES 4   **PREP** 15 minutes   **COOK** 10 minutes
½ teaspoon five-spice powder
¼ cup oyster sauce
2 tablespoons honey
2 tablespoons rice wine vinegar
2 garlic cloves, crushed
2cm piece fresh ginger, peeled, finely grated
600g pork fillets, thinly sliced
1 tablespoon vegetable oil
1 medium red onion, thickly sliced
1 bunch broccolini, roughly chopped
150g snow peas, trimmed, halved diagonally
500g baby choy sum, roughly chopped
Steamed jasmine rice, to serve

1 Combine five-spice, oyster sauce, honey, vinegar, garlic and ginger in a small bowl. Place pork and 1 tablespoon marinade in a medium bowl. Stir to coat.

2 Heat a wok over high heat. Add oil. Swirl to coat. Stir-fry pork, in batches, for 2 to 3 minutes or until just cooked through. Add remaining marinade, onion and broccolini. Stir-fry for 1 to 2 minutes or until onion softens. Add snow peas and choy sum. Stir-fry for 1 to 2 minutes or until choy sum just wilts. Serve with rice.

NUTRITION: (per serve) 1917kJ; 8.9g fat; 1.9g sat fat; 40.8g protein; 50.6g carbs; 4.1g fibre; 142mg chol; 837mg sodium.

low kilojoule, low saturated fat

SWEET POTATO & HAM FRITTERS

SERVES 4
PREP 25 minutes
COOK 24 minutes

500g orange sweet potato, peeled, grated
200g shaved leg ham, chopped
5 green onions, thinly sliced
½ cup chopped fresh flat-leaf parsley leaves
1 tablespoon dijon mustard
⅓ cup plain flour
1 large egg, lightly beaten
1 tablespoon olive oil
Mixed salad and tomato chutney, to serve

1 Preheat oven to 170°C/150°C fan-forced. Place a wire rack over a baking tray lined with baking paper.

2 Place potato, ham, onion, parsley, mustard and flour in a large bowl. Stir to combine. Season with pepper. Stir in egg.

3 Heat half the oil in a large non-stick frying pan over medium-high heat. Place ¼ cup mixture into pan, flatten slightly. Repeat to make 4 fritters. Cook for 3 to 4 minutes each side or until cooked through. Transfer fritters to prepared tray. Place in oven to keep warm. Repeat to make a total of 12 fritters.

4 Serve fritters with salad and chutney.

NUTRITION: (per serve) 1201kJ; 8.8g fat; 1.8g sat fat; 16.2g protein; 33.7g carbs; 3.9g fibre; 81mg chol; 973mg sodium.

Low saturated fat

PORK SAUSAGE STEW WITH ALMOND COUSCOUS

SERVES 4

PREP 15 minutes

COOK 30 minutes

1 tablespoon olive oil

8 thick pork sausages

1 large red onion, cut into wedges

2 teaspoons ground coriander

2 teaspoons ground cumin

800g canned diced tomatoes

270g jar chargrilled capsicums, drained

1½ cups chicken stock

1½ cups couscous

2 tablespoons slivered almonds, toasted

⅓ cup finely chopped fresh flat-leaf parsley leaves

100g reduced-fat fetta, crumbled

1 Heat oil in a large, deep frying pan over high heat. Cook sausages for 10 minutes or until browned all over and cooked through. Transfer to a plate lined with paper towel.

2 Add onion to pan. Cook, stirring, for 5 minutes or until softened. Add coriander and cumin. Cook, stirring, for 1 minute or until fragrant.

3 Add diced tomatoes, ½ cup cold water, capsicum and sausages. Bring to the boil. Reduce heat to medium-low. Cook for 10 minutes or until sauce thickens.

4 Meanwhile, bring stock to the boil over high heat. Place couscous in a large heatproof bowl. Add stock. Cover. Stand for 3 to 5 minutes or until liquid has absorbed. Stir with a fork to separate grains. Stir in almonds, parsley and fetta. Serve couscous with sausage stew.

NUTRITION: (per serve) 3583kJ; 45.6g fat; 16.7g sat fat; 41.1g protein; 67.9g carbs; 5.5g fibre; 100mg chol; 1936mg sodium.

High fibre

PORK & STRAWBERRY SALAD

SERVES 4　**PREP** 10 minutes　**COOK** 20 minutes

400g pork fillet
2 tablespoons olive oil
2 teaspoons cracked black pepper
⅓ cup balsamic vinegar
250g strawberries, hulled, halved
2 teaspoons lemon juice
80g salad leaves
50g goat's cheese, crumbled
1 tablespoon sunflower seeds

1 Heat a frying pan over medium-high heat. Drizzle pork with half the oil. Sprinkle with pepper and rub to coat. Cook pork, turning, for 12 to 15 minutes or until cooked through. Transfer to a plate. Stand covered for 5 minutes to rest. Reduce heat to low. Add balsamic vinegar to pan. Bring to a simmer. Simmer for 5 minutes or until reduced by half.

2 Place strawberries, balsamic vinegar and lemon juice in a bowl. Toss to combine.

3 Slice pork. Place salad leaves on a platter. Top with pork, strawberry mixture, goat's cheese and seeds. Serve.

NUTRITION: (per serve) 1176kj; fat 15.8g; sat fat 4g; protein 26.2g; carbs 5.9g; fibre 2.3g; chol 99mg; sodium 130 mg.

Gluten free, low saturated fat

PORK CUTLETS WITH HONEY MUSTARD SAUCE

SERVES 4　**PREP** 10 minutes　**COOK** 20 minutes

4 (800g) pork cutlets, trimmed
1 tablespoon olive oil
200g small button mushrooms
1 bunch spring onions, trimmed, halved
3 garlic cloves, thinly sliced
½ cup chicken stock
1½ cups frozen peas
2 tablespoons dijon mustard
2 tablespoons light thickened cream
1 tablespoon honey
2 teaspoons lemon juice
Mashed potato and lemon wedges, to serve

1 Season pork with salt and pepper. Heat half the oil in a large frying pan over medium-high heat. Cook pork for 4 minutes each side or until just cooked through. Set aside. Cover to keep warm.

2 Heat remaining oil in pan over medium-high heat. Add mushrooms, onion and garlic. Cook, stirring, for 5 minutes or until golden and tender. Add stock. Simmer, covered, for 3 minutes or until onion is just tender.

3 Add peas, mustard, cream and honey to pan. Season with salt and pepper. Stir to combine. Bring to boil. Boil for 1 minute or until sauce thickens slightly. Stir in juice.

4 Serve cutlets with vegetables, mashed potato and lemon wedges.

NUTRITION: (per serve) 2099kJ; 17.7g fat; 6.9g sat fat; 44.3g protein; 36.6g carbs; 8.4g fibre; 89mg chol; 580mg sodium.

Lower sodium

SAUSAGE

GRILLED APPLE & CHICKEN SAUSAGE SALAD

SERVES 4
PREP 15 minutes
COOK 10 minutes

8 chicken sausages
2 large red apples, cored, cut into thin wedges
150g baby spinach
1 Lebanese cucumber, cut into ribbons (see note)
½ small red onion, thinly sliced
2 tablespoons extra virgin olive oil
2 tablespoons apple cider vinegar
1 teaspoon wholegrain mustard
Crusty bread, to serve

1 Heat a greased barbecue hotplate and chargrill on medium-high heat. Cook sausages on hotplate for 5 to 6 minutes or until cooked through. Slice thickly. Cover.

2 Cook apple slices on chargrill for 1 to 2 minutes each side or until lightly charred.

3 Combine sausage, apple, spinach, cucumber and onion in a large bowl. Place oil, vinegar and mustard in a small bowl. Whisk until combined. Season with salt and pepper. Add dressing to salad. Toss gently to combine. Serve salad with bread.

NUTRITION: (per serve) 1756kJ; 20g fat; 4.4g sat fat; 15.9g protein; 42.8g carbs; 4.9g fibre; 21mg chol; 778mg sodium.

COOK'S NOTE Use a vegetable peeler to cut cucumber into thin ribbons.

Low saturated fat

CHORIZO, CHICKPEA & SPINACH STEW

SERVES 4
PREP 10 minutes
COOK 20 minutes

2 teaspoons olive oil
500g chorizo sausages
1 teaspoon smoked paprika
400g can diced tomatoes with basil and garlic
400g can chickpeas, drained, rinsed
80g baby spinach
4 slices sourdough bread, chargrilled, to serve

1 Heat oil in a large, deep frying pan over medium-high heat. Cook chorizo, turning, for 8 minutes. Transfer to a board. Slice.

2 Add paprika to pan. Cook for 1 minute or until fragrant. Return sausages to pan with tomato, chickpeas and ½ cup cold water. Simmer, covered, over medium-high heat for 10 minutes or until sausages are cooked through. Remove from heat. Stir in spinach.

3 Serve stew with chargrilled bread.

NUTRITION: (per serve) 3279kJ; 44.5g fat; 17.4g sat fat; 41g protein; 52.2g carbs; 8.2g fibre; 60mg chol; 2705mg sodium.

High fibre

THAI YELLOW CURRY WITH BEEF SAUSAGE

SERVES 4
PREP 10 minutes
COOK 25 minutes

1½ cups jasmine rice
2 teaspoons vegetable oil
500g packet beef with garlic and parsley sausages
2 tablespoons Thai yellow curry paste
400ml can coconut milk
3 cups (300g) frozen Thai-style stir-fry vegetables
⅓ cup fresh coriander leaves

1 Rinse rice well under cold running water. Place rice and 1½ cups cold water in a large saucepan. Cover. Bring to the boil over high heat. Reduce heat to medium-low. Simmer, partially covered, for 12 to 15 minutes or until liquid is absorbed. Remove from heat. Stand for 5 minutes. Season with salt and pepper. Fluff rice with a fork to separate grains.

2 Meanwhile, heat oil in a large, deep frying pan over medium-high heat. Cook sausages, turning, for 8 to 10 minutes or until browned and just cooked through. Transfer to a board. Thickly slice.

3 Drain oil from pan leaving 1 teaspoon oil. Reduce heat to medium. Add curry paste. Cook, stirring, for 1 minute or until fragrant. Add coconut milk. Bring to a simmer.

4 Return sausages to pan. Add vegetables. Simmer for a further 3 to 4 minutes or until heated through. Serve curry spooned over rice and topped with coriander leaves.

NUTRITION: (per serve) 3518kJ; 47.8g fat; 31.2g sat fat; 24.3g protein; 76.7g carbs; 6g fibre; 54mg chol; 1244mg sodium.

CHICKEN MEATBALLS WITH CREAMY MUSTARD SAUCE

SERVES 4　　**PREP** 10 minutes　　**COOK** 20 minutes

500g lean chicken sausages
1 tablespoon olive oil
1 small red onion, finely chopped
2 garlic cloves, crushed
250g button mushrooms, thinly sliced
1 tablespoon plain flour
1 cup chicken stock
300ml pure cream
2 tablespoons wholegrain mustard
2 tablespoons chopped fresh chives
Cooked penne pasta and steamed broccoli, to serve

1 Squeeze chicken from sausage casings into a bowl. Roll level tablespoons into balls. Heat half the oil in a large frying pan over medium heat. Add meatballs. Cook, turning, for 4 to 5 minutes or until browned and cooked through. Transfer to a plate lined with paper towel. Wipe pan clean.

2 Return pan to heat. Add remaining oil to pan. Add onion. Cook, stirring, for 3 to 5 minutes or until softened. Add garlic and mushrooms. Cook, stirring, for 5 minutes or until mushrooms are tender.

3 Sprinkle flour into pan. Stir for 1 minute. Add stock, cream and mustard. Stir until well combined. Reduce heat to medium-low. Cook for 4 to 5 minutes or until sauce has thickened slightly. Return meatballs to pan with half the chives. Season with salt and pepper. Cook for 1 minute or until heated through.

4 Divide pasta between bowls. Spoon over meatball mixture. Sprinkle with remaining chives. Serve with broccoli.

NUTRITION: (per serve) 2810kJ; 44.9g fat; 22.8g sat fat; 29.3g protein; 34.9g carbs; 6.3g fibre; 107mg chol; 1136mg sodium.

COOK'S NOTE You could use other sausages, such as pork or lamb, in this dish.

ITALIAN SAUSAGE & CAPSICUM PIZZA

SERVES 4　　**PREP** 10 minutes　　**COOK** 10 minutes

3 (225g) thick Italian-style beef sausages
2 x 150g pizza bases
Olive oil cooking spray
⅔ cup tomato and basil pasta sauce
1 cup grated mozzarella cheese
1 cup roasted capsicum strips
25g baby rocket

1 Heat a greased barbecue hotplate or chargrill (with hood) on medium heat. Remove sausage mince from casings. Break mince into 2cm pieces.

2 Spray both sides of each pizza base with oil. Place bases on barbecue. Cook one side of each base for 2 minutes or until golden and crisp. Remove from barbecue. Place each base, cooked-side up, on a double layer of greased foil.

3 Spread sauce evenly over bases. Sprinkle evenly with cheese. Top with capsicum and sausage mince. Return pizzas, on foil, to barbecue. Close hood. Cook for 6 to 8 minutes or until mince is cooked and bases are golden and crisp. Cut into wedges. Sprinkle with rocket. Serve.

NUTRITION: (per serve) 1904kJ; 23g fat; 9.5g sat fat; 22.9g protein; 38.8g carbs; 2.5g fibre; 48mg chol; 1131mg sodium.

SAUSAGE & COUSCOUS SALAD

SERVES 4
PREP 10 minutes
COOK 12 minutes

2 teaspoons vegetable oil
3 (230g) thick beef and red wine sausages
1½ cups couscous
100g snow peas, trimmed, thinly sliced diagonally
250g cherry tomatoes, halved
¼ cup fresh basil leaves, torn
¼ cup balsamic salad dressing

1 Heat oil in a large heavy-based frying pan over medium-high heat. Cook sausages, turning, for 8 to 10 minutes or until sausages are browned and cooked through. Transfer to a board. Cut sausages diagonally into 1cm-thick slices.

2 Meanwhile, place couscous in a large heatproof bowl. Stir in 1½ cups boiling water. Cover. Set aside for 5 minutes or until liquid has absorbed. Using a fork, fluff couscous to separate grains.

3 Add sausage, snow pea, tomato and basil to couscous. Season with salt and pepper. Toss to combine. Drizzle with dressing. Serve.

NUTRITION: (per serve) 2124kj; fat 21.7g; sat fat 5.5g; protein 16.8g; carbs 59.8g; fibre 2.5g; chol 18mg; sodium 570 mg.

WARM SAUSAGE, POTATO & SPINACH SALAD

SERVES 4
PREP 5 minutes
COOK 30 minutes

400g packet baby potatoes with butter and herbs (see note)
500g Italian beef sausages
100g baby spinach
⅓ cup balsamic and roasted garlic salad dressing
¾ cup pitted black olives
¼ cup pine nuts, toasted
Crusty bread, to serve

1 Cook potatoes following packet directions, until just tender. Set aside for 5 minutes to cool slightly.

2 Meanwhile, heat a chargrill pan over medium-high heat. Cook sausages for 10 minutes, turning, or until browned and cooked through. Transfer to a plate. Set aside for 5 minutes to cool slightly. Slice diagonally.

3 Thickly slice potatoes. Arrange spinach, potato and sausage on plates. Drizzle with salad dressing. Sprinkle with olives and pine nuts. Season with pepper. Serve with crusty bread.

NUTRITION: (per serve) 2645kj; fat 38.3g; sat fat 15.3g; protein 26.9g; carbs 43.7g; fibre 4.4g; chol 94mg; sodium 2479 mg.

COOK'S NOTE Baby potatoes with butter and herbs are available in the fresh fruit and vegetable section of the supermarket.

DESSERT

MICROWAVE MOCHA SELF-SAUCING PUDDINGS

We used a 1000-watt microwave for this recipe.

SERVES 4   **PREP** 5 minutes   **COOK** 5 minutes

¾ cup self-raising flour, sifted
1 tablespoon cocoa powder, sifted
1 teaspoon instant espresso powder
½ cup caster sugar
60g butter, melted
½ cup milk
Double cream, to serve
Sauce
2 teaspoons cornflour
1 tablespoon cocoa powder, sifted
1 teaspoon instant espresso powder
¼ cup brown sugar
¾ cup boiling water

1 Combine flour, cocoa powder, espresso powder, caster sugar, butter and milk in a bowl. Stir until smooth. Spoon into four 1¼ cup-capacity heatproof, microwave-safe dishes.

2 Make Sauce Combine cornflour, cocoa powder, espresso powder, brown sugar and boiling water in a heatproof jug. Stir until smooth. Gently pour sauce evenly over batter in each dish.

3 Place dishes on microwave turntable. Microwave on MEDIUM-HIGH (75%) for 5 minutes or until tops are firm to touch. Stand for 1 minute. Dollop with cream. Serve.

NUTRITION: (per serve) 1975kJ; 24.4g fat; 15.8g sat fat; 4.9g protein; 60g carbs; 1.2g fibre; 69mg chol; 318mg sodium.

PEAR & CHERRY JAM GALETTES

SERVES 4   **PREP** 3 minutes   **COOK** 7 minutes

1 sheet frozen puff pastry, partially thawed
2 tablespoons cherry berry jam
½ x 410g can pear slices in fruit juice, drained, halved (see note)
½ teaspoon cinnamon sugar
Vanilla ice-cream, to serve

1 Preheat oven to 240°C/220°C fan-forced. Line a large baking tray with baking paper.

2 Cut pastry sheet into 4 even squares. Leaving a 1.5cm border around edges, spread pastry squares with the jam. Top each square with the sliced pear, slightly overlapping. Sprinkle with cinnamon sugar.

3 Bake for 7 minutes or until golden and puffed. Serve with ice-cream.

NUTRITION: (per serve) 1209kJ; 11.8g fat; 6.5g sat fat; 3.9g protein; 41g carbs; 1.5g fibre; 15mg chol; 184mg sodium.

MICROWAVE CHOCOLATE FUDGE CAKE

SERVES 8
PREP 3 minutes
COOK 7 minutes
1 cup caster sugar
¼ cup cocoa powder, sifted
1½ cups self-raising flour
½ cup walnut crumbs
2 eggs
¾ cup milk
125g butter, melted
Vanilla ice-cream, to serve
Sauce
180g dark chocolate
⅓ cup thickened cream

1 Grease a 20cm-square microwave-safe dish. Line base and sides with baking paper.

2 Combine sugar, cocoa, flour and walnuts in a bowl. Add eggs, milk and butter. Mix well to combine. Pour mixture into dish.

3 Microwave on MEDIUM-HIGH (75%) for 6 to 7 minutes or until just firm to touch.

4 Meanwhile, make Sauce Place chocolate and cream in a small saucepan over medium heat. Cook, stirring, for 2 minutes or until smooth.

5 Turn cake onto a baking paper-lined wire rack. Carefully cut into 8 pieces. Drizzle with sauce. Serve with ice-cream.

NUTRITION: (per serve) 2621kJ; 35.8g fat; 18.3g sat fat; 9.3g protein; 69.7g carbs; 2.1g fibre; 104mg chol; 361mg sodium.

STICKY MAPLE PEARS WITH TOASTED MADEIRA CAKE

SERVES 4
PREP 5 minutes
COOK 5 minutes
20g butter
2 large beurre bosc pears, peeled, cored, cut into thin wedges
½ cup maple syrup
8 thick slices madeira cake
Double cream, to serve

1 Preheat grill on high.

2 Melt butter in a large frying pan over medium-high heat. Cook pears for 2 minutes, turning. Add maple syrup and 1 tablespoon cold water. Bring to a simmer. Reduce heat to low. Simmer, turning occasionally, for 3 minutes or until sauce thickens and pears are soft.

3 Meanwhile, place cake slices under grill. Cook slices for 1 minute each side or until golden and toasted.

4 Divide cake between serving plates. Top with pears and drizzle with sauce. Serve dolloped with cream.

NUTRITION: (per serve) 2963kJ; 27.5g fat; 11g sat fat; 6.7g protein; 108.8g carbs; 3.3g fibre; 62mg chol; 597mg sodium.

MICROWAVE BREAD & BUTTER PUDDING

We used a 1100-watt microwave oven for this recipe

SERVES 4

PREP 10 minutes (plus 10 minutes standing time)

COOK 15 minutes

5 slices spicy fruit bread
50g butter, softened
¼ cup dried figs, quartered (see note)
2 egg yolks
4 eggs
1 cup milk
½ cup caster sugar
1 teaspoon vanilla extract
Icing sugar mixture, to serve

1 Spread both sides of bread with butter. Cut into quarters to make triangles. Arrange bread triangles, slightly overlapping, in a 5-cup-capacity, 16cm x 25cm heatproof, microwave-safe dish. Sprinkle with figs.

2 Whisk egg yolks, eggs, milk, caster sugar and vanilla together in a large jug. Pour egg mixture over bread. Press bread down gently into egg mixture. Set aside for 10 minutes to allow egg mixture to be absorbed.

3 Microwave, uncovered, on MEDIUM (50%) for 10 minutes or until egg mixture has just set.

4 Meanwhile, preheat grill on medium. Place bread and butter pudding under grill. Grill for 5 minutes or until top is golden. Serve dusted with icing sugar.

NUTRITION: (per serve) 2046kJ; 21.3g fat; 10.8g sat fat; 13.7g protein; 61g carbs; 1.6g fibre; 317mg chol; 297mg sodium.

LIME & COCONUT RICE WITH SUGARED PINEAPPLE

We used a 1100-watt microwave oven for this recipe

SERVES 4

PREP 5 minutes

COOK 21 minutes

1 cup long grain white rice
400ml can coconut milk
½ cup caster sugar
2 teaspoons finely grated lime rind
1 tablespoon lime juice
½ teaspoon vanilla extract
¼ cup firmly packed brown sugar
3 x 5mm-thick slices fresh pineapple, quartered
Whipped cream and lime zest, to serve

1 Place rice in a 2.2 litre microwave rice cooker. Add 2 cups boiling water. Microwave, covered, on HIGH (100%) for 12 minutes or until water is absorbed.

2 Add coconut milk and caster sugar. Microwave, covered, on HIGH (100%) for 5 minutes. Stir. Microwave, uncovered, on HIGH (100%) for 3 to 4 minutes or until mixture has thickened. Stir in lime rind, juice and vanilla.

3 Place brown sugar in a shallow bowl. Dip pineapple in sugar, coating both sides. Serve rice pudding with pineapple, cream and sprinkled with lime zest.

NUTRITION: (per serve) 2798kJ; 20.7g fat; 16.5g sat fat; 5.5g protein; 117g carbs; 2.6g fibre; 21mg chol; 26mg sodium.

STUFFED PEARS WITH BUTTERSCOTCH SAUCE

We used a 1100-watt microwave oven for this recipe

SERVES 4

PREP 10 minutes

COOK 13 minutes (plus 2 minutes standing time)

10g butter, softened

¼ cup pecans, finely chopped

¼ cup sultanas

¼ teaspoon ground cinnamon

1 tablespoon brown sugar

4 medium packham pears, peeled (see note)

Pure cream, to serve

Butterscotch sauce

100g butter, chopped

½ cup firmly packed brown sugar

½ cup thickened cream

1 Using fingers, rub butter, pecans, sultanas, cinnamon and sugar together until well combined.

2 Cut tops off pears, about one-third from the top of each pear. Leaving a 1cm border around edge, use a teaspoon to scoop out a 3cm-deep hole from cut side of each pear base. Discard flesh. Divide pecan mixture between holes.

3 Make Butterscotch sauce Place butter into a deep, 3 litre-capacity heatproof, microwave-safe dish. Cover. Microwave on HIGH (100%) for 1 minute or until butter has melted. Add brown sugar and cream. Whisk to combine.

4 Place pears and pear tops into the sauce. Cover loosely with plastic wrap. Microwave on HIGH (100%) for 7 minutes or until pears are soft but still holding their shape. Carefully remove pear bases from sauce and place in serving bowls. Top with pear tops. Microwave sauce, uncovered, on HIGH (100%) for 5 minutes or until slightly thickened. Stand sauce for 2 minutes. Spoon sauce over pears. Serve with cream.

NUTRITION: (per serve) 2710kJ; 49.1g fat; 28.9g sat fat; 2.6g protein; 52g carbs; 2.6g fibre; 128mg chol; 224mg sodium.

COOK'S NOTE Trim a small amount off the base of each pear if they don't sit flat in dish.

CHOCOLATE SALTED CARAMEL MUG CAKES

We used a 1100-watt microwave oven for this recipe

SERVES 4

PREP 5 minutes

COOK 4 minutes

½ cup self-raising flour
½ cup caster sugar
⅓ cup cocoa powder, sifted
1 egg
½ cup milk
1½ tablespoons vegetable oil
1 teaspoon salt
6 jersey caramels, quartered
Double cream, to serve

1 Whisk flour, sugar, cocoa, egg, milk and oil together in a medium bowl. Divide mixture between four 1-cup-capacity, microwave-safe mugs.

2 Microwave on HIGH (100%) for 1 minute. Top with half the salt and half the caramel. Microwave on HIGH (100%) for a further 1 minute. Top with remaining salt and caramels. Microwave on HIGH (100%) for a further 2 minutes or until cakes spring back when lightly pressed. Serve dolloped with cream.

NUTRITION: (per serve) 1647kJ; 18.4g fat; 7.9g sat fat; 6.4g protein; 52.4g carbs; 1.2g fibre; 74mg chol; 906mg sodium.

MANGO, COCONUT & BANANA PARFAITS

SERVES 4
PREP 10 minutes
250g butternut snap biscuits
⅓ cup coconut milk
1 large mango, chopped
1 large banana, chopped
1½ cups vanilla yoghurt
Extra chopped mango, to serve

1 Place biscuits in a food processor. Process until coarse crumbs form. Set aside.

2 Blend coconut milk, mango and banana in a blender until smooth. Transfer to a bowl. Fold through yoghurt until just marbled.

3 Reserve 2 tablespoons of biscuit mixture. Divide half the remaining biscuit mixture between four 1½ cup-capacity serving glasses. Top with half the yoghurt mixture. Repeat layers. Serve topped with the extra mango and reserved biscuit mixture.

NUTRITION: (per serve) 2271kJ; 20.7g fat; 14.6g sat fat; 9.9g protein; 75.5g carbs; 5.3g fibre; 28mg chol; 396mg sodium.

CHOC-CARAMEL ICE-CREAM CUPS

SERVES 4
PREP 8 minutes
COOK 1 minute
1½ cups vanilla ice-cream
100g milk chocolate, chopped
¼ cup thickened cream
200g packet caramel-filled chocolate biscuits, chopped
4 dark chocolate dessert cups (see note)
1 tablespoon toasted slivered almonds

1 Place ice-cream in a bowl. Set aside for 5 minutes to soften.

2 Meanwhile, place chocolate and cream in a heatproof, microwave-safe bowl. Microwave on HIGH (100%) for 1 minute 30 seconds, stirring every 30 seconds, or until melted and smooth.

3 Add biscuits to ice-cream. Fold to combine. Scoop ice-cream mixture into chocolate cups. Drizzle with chocolate sauce. Sprinkle with almonds. Serve.

NUTRITION: (per serve) 2672kJ; 35.4g fat; 21g sat fat; 8.4g protein; 72.6g carbs; 1.2g fibre; 33mg chol; 137mg sodium.

COOK'S NOTE Dark chocolate dessert cups are in the ready-made cake aisle of supermarkets.

10-MINUTE HONEY CHEESECAKES

MAKES 12
PREP 10 minutes
2 butternut snap biscuits
250g block cream cheese, softened
¼ cup honey
12 shortcrust pastry tartlets (see note)
300ml thickened cream, whipped

1 Place biscuits in a small food processor. Pulse until fine crumbs form.

2 Using an electric mixer, beat cream cheese and honey until smooth.

3 Spoon cheese mixture between pastry cases. Spoon cream into a piping bag fitted with a 1cm fluted nozzle. Pipe cream over cream cheese mixture. Sprinkle with the biscuit crumbs. Serve immediately.

NUTRITION: (each) 1175kJ; 21.8g fat; 13.4g sat fat; 3.4g protein; 18.6g carbs; 0.4g fibre; 53mg chol; 226mg sodium.

COOK'S NOTE We used 2 x 150g packets pastry tartlets from the bakery section of the supermarket.

CHOCOLATE & SALTED CARAMEL ICE-CREAM STACKS

SERVES 12
PREP 5 minutes
COOK 1 minute
500g bought chocolate block cake
1 cup toffee sauce
2 teaspoons sea salt flakes
12 scoops honey macadamia ice-cream

1 Cut cake into 12 pieces. Arrange on serving plates.

2 Place sauce in a small saucepan over high heat. Heat for 1 minute or until sauce begins to simmer. Remove from heat. Stir in salt.

3 Place 1 scoop of ice-cream onto each cake. Drizzle over hot sauce. Serve immediately.

NUTRITION: (per serve) 1527kJ; 20.4g fat; 11.2g sat fat; 4.4g protein; 42.1g carbs; 0.7g fibre; 56mg chol; 403mg sodium.

MICROWAVE ORANGE & ALMOND SYRUP CAKE

We used a 1000-watt microwave for this recipe
SERVES 8
PREP 3 minutes
COOK 7 minutes
¾ cup self-raising flour
½ cup caster sugar
½ cup almond meal
¼ cup orange juice (see note)
2 tablespoons vegetable oil
1 egg, lightly beaten
¼ cup milk
Double cream, to serve
Orange syrup
1 cup orange juice
⅓ cup caster sugar

1 Grease a 7cm-deep, 8cm x 19cm microwave-safe silicone loaf pan. Line base and sides with baking paper.

2 Combine flour, sugar, almond meal, orange juice, oil, egg and milk in a bowl. Pour into prepared pan. Microwave on HIGH (100%) for 6 to 7 minutes or until top is firm to touch.

3 Meanwhile, make Orange syrup Combine the orange juice, sugar and 2 tablespoons cold water in a saucepan over medium heat. Bring to a simmer, stirring occasionally. Simmer for 2 minutes.

4 Turn cake out onto a baking paper-lined wire rack over a tray. Drizzle half the syrup over the top of the cake. Serve cake warm with remaining syrup and a dollop of cream.

NUTRITION: (per serve) 1200kJ; 14.3g fat; 4.4g sat fat; 4.1g protein; 36.1g carbs; 1.2g fibre; 37mg chol; 107mg sodium.

COOK'S NOTE We used bottled fresh orange juice to save time.

BANOFFEE MERINGUE MESS

SERVES 4
PREP 10 minutes
½ cup toffee dessert sauce
2 large bananas, thinly sliced
8 pavlova nests, roughly broken
300ml tub thickened cream, whipped
Grated dark chocolate, to serve

1 Microwave sauce on HIGH (100%) for 10 seconds or until just heated through, but not hot. Toss banana in sauce to coat. Fold meringue and cream together until just combined.

2 Spoon half the banana mixture between 4 x 1½ cup-capacity serving glasses. Top with half the cream mixture. Repeat layers. Sprinkle with chocolate. Serve.

NUTRITION: (per serve) 1902kJ; 31.1g fat; 19.8g sat fat; 3.7g protein; 41.1g carbs; 1.4g fibre; 82mg chol; 53mg sodium.

POACHED RHUBARB WITH GINGER PECAN CRUMBLE

SERVES 4
PREP 5 minutes
COOK 5 minutes
⅓ cup caster sugar
2 tablespoons orange juice
1 bunch rhubarb, trimmed, cut into 4cm pieces
6 gingernut biscuits
¼ cup pecan nuts
Vanilla ice-cream, to serve

1 Combine sugar, ⅓ cup cold water and juice in a saucepan over medium heat. Cook, stirring, until sugar is dissolved. Bring to a simmer. Add rhubarb. Reduce heat to low. Simmer for 5 minutes or until tender. Remove from heat.

2 Meanwhile, process biscuits and pecans in a small food processor until coarse crumbs.

3 Divide rhubarb between 4 serving bowls. Sprinkle with crumble. Serve with ice-cream.

NUTRITION: (per serve) 1354kJ; 12g fat; 4.4g sat fat; 3.8g protein; 49g carbs; 2.8g fibre; 6mg chol; 89mg sodium.

BANANA BREAD TRIFLES

SERVES 4
PREP 10 minutes
5 thick slices (500g packet) banana bread,
   cut into 2cm cubes
1 cup premium vanilla custard
⅓ cup mixed berry dessert sauce
Double cream, to serve

1 Divide half the banana bread between 4 x 1¼ cup-capacity serving glasses. Top with half the custard and half the sauce. Repeat layers.

2 Top trifles with double cream. Serve.

NUTRITION: (per serve) 2620kJ; 28g fat; 13g sat fat; 9.1g protein; 81.7g carbs; 3.3g fibre; 52mg chol; 395mg sodium.

CHOC-FUDGE KNICKERBOCKER GLORY

SERVES 4
PREP 10 minutes

8 scoops vanilla ice-cream
⅓ cup chocolate dessert sauce
250g strawberries, hulled, sliced (see note)
¾ cup thickened cream, whipped
Chocolate sprinkles, to decorate

1 Divide half the ice-cream between 4 serving glasses. Drizzle with half the chocolate sauce and add half the strawberries. Repeat layers.

2 Dollop whipped cream over strawberries. Top with chocolate sprinkles. Serve.

NUTRITION: (per serve) 1974kJ; 30g fat; 18.2g sat fat; 5.2g protein; 44.9g carbs; 1.3g fibre; 59mg chol; 90mg sodium.

COOK'S NOTE If strawberries aren't in season, use frozen berries instead.

10-MINUTE APPLE BERRY CRUMBLE

SERVES 4
PREP 10 minutes
COOK 3 minutes

2 x 400g cans apple pie filling
1 teaspoon ground cinnamon
1 teaspoon finely grated lemon rind
2 tablespoons mixed berry jam
1 cup toasted muesli
Double cream, to serve

1 Combine apple, cinnamon and lemon rind in a bowl. Divide jam between 4 x 1¼ cup-capacity heatproof, microwave-safe dishes. Top with apple mixture. Cover with plastic wrap. Microwave on HIGH (100%) for 2½ minutes or until heated through.

2 Sprinkle muesli on top of apple mixture. Microwave on MEDIUM (50%), uncovered, for 15 to 20 seconds or until muesli is just warm. Serve hot with double cream.

NUTRITION: (per serve) 1534kJ; 13.2g fat; 7.5g sat fat; 3.5g protein; 58.8g carbs; 4.8g fibre; 26mg chol; 132mg sodium.

BALSAMIC & VANILLA STRAWBERRIES

SERVES 4
PREP 20 minutes
2 tablespoons icing sugar mixture
2 tablespoons balsamic vinegar
1 vanilla bean, split
500g strawberries, hulled, halved
1 cup reduced-fat vanilla yoghurt

1 Combine sugar and vinegar in a bowl. Scrape seeds from half of the vanilla bean. Add to sugar mixture. Stir to combine. Add strawberries. Toss to coat. Refrigerate for 10 minutes.

2 Place yoghurt in a bowl. Scrape seeds from remaining vanilla bean half. Add to yoghurt. Stir to combine. Serve strawberries with yoghurt mixture and vinegar mixture.

NUTRITION: (per serve) 501kj; fat 1.2g; sat fat 0.7g; protein 5.4g; carbs 20.5g; fibre 2.7g; chol 7mg; sodium 54 mg.

Low fat, low in kilojoules

APPLE TARTE TATIN

SERVES 4
PREP 5 minutes
COOK 25 minutes
50g unsalted butter
4 medium green apples, peeled, cored, quartered
½ cup brown sugar
1 sheet frozen puff pastry, partially thawed
Double cream, to serve

1 Preheat oven to 220°C/200°C fan-forced. Grease a 6cm-deep, 20cm-round (base) cake pan. Line base with baking paper.

2 Melt butter in a large frying pan over medium-high heat. Add apple. Cook, turning, for 3 to 4 minutes or until golden. Add sugar and 2 tablespoons cold water. Cook, stirring, for 2 to 3 minutes or until sugar has dissolved. Bring to the boil. Reduce heat to low. Simmer for 2 to 3 minutes or until slightly thickened.

3 Arrange apple in prepared pan. Spoon over sugar mixture. Cut a 22cm round from pastry. Place pastry over apple, tucking in at edge. Bake for 12 to 15 minutes or until golden and puffed. Stand in pan for 5 minutes. Turn out onto a plate. Serve with cream.

NUTRITION: (per serve) 1813kj; fat 25.6g; sat fat 15.8g; protein 2.8g; carbs 48.7g; fibre 3g; chol 52mg; sodium 128 mg.

BERRY CHEESECAKE PARFAITS

SERVES 4   **PREP** 25 minutes
250g reduced-fat cream cheese
¼ cup caster sugar
170g tub 98% fat-free berry yoghurt
300g frozen mixed berries, thawed
150g packet almond biscotti, chopped

1 Using an electric mixer, beat cheese and sugar until smooth. Mix in yoghurt and ¼ cup berries until just combined.

2 Divide ⅔ cup remaining berries between four 2 cup-capacity glasses. Sprinkle with half the biscotti. Spoon 2 tablespoons cheese mixture into each glass. Repeat layers, finishing with berries. Serve.

NUTRITION: (per serve) 1824kj; fat 19.4g; sat fat 10.7g; protein 11.2g; carbs 54.4g; fibre 3.4g; chol 33mg; sodium 292 mg.

MAPLE PEARS WITH BUTTERNUT ICE-CREAM

SERVES 4   **PREP** 14 minutes   **COOK** 7 minutes
1 litre vanilla ice-cream, slightly softened
8 butternut snap cookies, finely chopped
25g unsalted butter, chopped
4 corella pears, halved
¼ cup maple syrup

1 Place ice-cream in a large metal bowl. Add cookies. Stir to combine. Cover surface with plastic wrap, then foil. Freeze for 10 minutes.

2 Meanwhile, melt butter in a frying pan over medium-high heat. Add pear, cut-side down. Cook for 2 to 3 minutes or until golden. Turn. Add maple syrup. Bring to the boil. Reduce heat to low. Simmer for 3 to 4 minutes or until pears have just softened.

3 Serve pears with ice-cream mixture and maple syrup mixture.

NUTRITION: (per serve) 2488kj; fat 24.8g; sat fat 16.6g; protein 6g; carbs 86g; fibre 5.1g; chol 34mg; sodium 221 mg.

MANDARIN & GINGER PANCAKES WITH PECANS

SERVES 4   **PREP** 5 minutes   **COOK** 5 minutes

20g butter
½ teaspoon ground ginger
2 tablespoons caster sugar
2 tablespoons fresh mandarin juice (see notes)
3 mandarins, segmented
6 ready-made fresh pancakes, halved, warmed (see notes)
¼ cup sour cream
¼ cup chopped pecans, toasted
Icing sugar, for dusting

1 Melt butter in a small frying pan over medium-low heat. Add ginger. Cook for 30 seconds or until fragrant. Add sugar and mandarin juice. Cook for 1 minute or until reduced slightly. Add mandarin segments. Cook for 1 minute or until heated through.

2 Spread each pancake half with sour cream. Divide mandarin mixture and pecans evenly between pancake halves. Fold to enclose. Serve dusted with icing sugar.

NUTRITION: (per serve) 2230kJ; 26.8g fat; 12g sat fat; 6.9g protein; 64.9g carbs; 3.6g fibre; 60mg chol; 415mg sodium.

COOK'S NOTES You need 1 large mandarin for the mandarin juice. We used pancakes from the bakery section of the supermarket.

High fibre

CARAMEL BANANA TRIFLE

SERVES 6   **PREP** 15 minutes

380g can caramel Top 'n' Fill
600ml thickened cream
2 tablespoons icing sugar mixture
1 teaspoon vanilla essence
225g rectangular unfilled sponge cake (see notes)
2 tablespoons coffee liqueur (optional, see notes)
3 large bananas, thinly sliced
⅓ cup dry-roasted hazelnuts, chopped

1 Place caramel and 1 cup cream in a bowl. Whisk until smooth. Using an electric mixer, beat icing sugar, vanilla and remaining cream for 3 minutes until soft peaks form.

2 Cut cake into 3cm pieces. Arrange half over the base of an 8 cup-capacity bowl. Drizzle half the liqueur, if using, over cake. Spoon half the caramel mixture over cake. Top with half the banana and half the cream mixture. Repeat layers with remaining cake, liqueur, caramel mixture, banana and cream mixture, finishing with cream mixture. Sprinkle with nuts. Serve.

NUTRITION: (per serve) 3298kj; fat 49.1g; sat fat 27.9g; protein 11.1g; carbs 72.5g; fibre 2.4g; chol 121mg; sodium 313 mg.

COOK'S NOTES Rectangular sponge cake is available in packs of 2 from supermarkets. Freeze remaining sponge for up to 2 months. You could use 1 teaspoon instant espresso coffee powder dissolved in 2 tablespoons boiling water instead of liqueur.

CHOC-HAZELNUT CREPE CAKE

SERVES 12
PREP 20 minutes (plus 15 minutes refrigeration)
COOK 3 minutes

2 x 180g blocks dark chocolate, chopped
⅔ cup thickened cream
3 x 400g packets (24 crepes) frozen French-style crepes, thawed
3 cups chocolate hazelnut spread
Chopped dry-roasted hazelnuts, to decorate
Whipped or double cream, to serve

1 Place chocolate and cream in a heatproof, microwave-safe bowl. Microwave on MEDIUM-HIGH (75%) for 2 to 3 minutes, stirring every 30 seconds with a metal spoon, until smooth. Refrigerate ganache for 15 minutes or until thick and spreadable.

2 Meanwhile, place 1 crepe on a serving plate. Spread with 1 heaped tablespoon of spread. Repeat with remaining crepes and spread, finishing with a crepe.

3 Spread ganache over cake sides and top. Sprinkle with hazelnuts. Serve with cream.

NUTRITION: (per serve) 2910kJ; 39.9g fat; 17.3g sat fat; 9.1g protein; 76.7g carbs; 1.6g fibre; 37mg chol; 345mg sodium.

COOK'S NOTES Cake can be made a day ahead. Store in the fridge. Stand at room temperature for 30 minutes before serving.

PINEAPPLE & COCONUT TART

SERVES 4
PREP 5 minutes
COOK 2 minutes

440g can crushed pineapple
1 tablespoon caster sugar
¼ teaspoon ground cinnamon
160g ready-made fresh pastry case (see note)
1½ tablespoons shredded coconut
1½ tablespoons flaked almonds
Double cream, to serve

1 Preheat grill on medium.

2 Strain pineapple through a fine sieve, pushing with the back of a spoon to remove excess liquid. Place pineapple in a bowl. Add sugar and cinnamon. Combine. Spoon mixture into pastry case. Top with coconut and almonds. Grill for 2 minutes or until top is lightly browned. Serve with cream.

NUTRITION: (per serve) 1576kJ; 22g fat; 11.9g sat fat; 3.5g protein; 40.7g carbs; 2.1g fibre; 36mg chol; 107mg sodium.

COOK'S NOTE We used a cooked pastry case from the bakery section of the supermarket.

RASPBERRY HONEY DESSERT CAKE

SERVES 12
PREP 10 minutes
2 cups thickened cream
1 tablespoon icing sugar mixture
2 x 125g punnets fresh raspberries
460g packet double unfilled sponge cakes
⅓ cup honey, warmed
2 tablespoons pistachio kernels, chopped

1 Using an electric mixer, beat cream and icing sugar together until medium peaks. Add ⅔ of the raspberries. Beat until mixture is combined and raspberries are roughly chopped.

2 Using a serrated knife, cut each sponge in half. Place one cake on serving plate. Brush liberally with honey. Top with ¼ cream mixture. Repeat layering, finishing with a layer of cream. Sprinkle with remaining raspberries and pistachios. Serve.

NUTRITION: (per serve) 1321kJ; 19.3g fat; 10.8g sat fat; 4.1g protein; 31.3g carbs; 1.4g fibre; 45mg chol; 248mg sodium.

MOCHA ICE-CREAM SUNDAES

SERVES 4
PREP 8 minutes
COOK 2 minutes
1 double shot (60ml) espresso, cooled
¼ cup thickened cream
100g dark chocolate, chopped
8 scoops vanilla ice-cream
½ cup mini white marshmallows
Mini chocolate wafer sticks, to serve

1 Combine espresso and cream in a heatproof, microwave-safe bowl. Add chocolate. Microwave on MEDIUM (50%) for 2 minutes or until mixture is smooth, stirring with a metal spoon halfway during cooking. Set aside for 2 minutes to cool slightly.

2 Place half of the ice-cream in serving glasses. Drizzle with half of the chocolate sauce. Sprinkle with half the marshmallows. Repeat layers. Serve ice-cream topped with wafers.

NUTRITION: (per serve) 2004kJ; 26.4g fat; 16g sat fat; 5.3g protein; 56.3g carbs; 0.3g fibre; 28mg chol; 130mg sodium.

RASPBERRY, MINT & APPLE SORBET

SERVES 4
PREP 5 minutes
500g packet frozen raspberries (see note)
2 tablespoons fresh mint leaves, torn
1½ cups chilled apple juice
Extra fresh mint leaves, to serve

1 Place raspberries, mint leaves and 1 cup apple juice in a food processor. Process, gradually adding remaining apple juice, until smooth and combined, scraping down sides of processor occasionally.

2 Working quickly, scoop mixture into serving glasses. Serve sprinkled with extra mint leaves.

NUTRITION: (per serve) 425kJ; 0.7g fat; 0.01g sat fat; 1.8g protein; 17.6g carbs; 7.2g fibre; 0mg chol; 8mg sodium.

COOK'S NOTE If you don't like the raspberry seeds, push the mixture through a sieve. You will then need to freeze the mixture for around 10 minutes to allow it to firm up again.

Low fat, gluten free, low kilojoule

LIME & COCONUT CHEESECAKE POTS

SERVES 4
PREP 10 minutes
½ x 250g packet butternut snap biscuits
2 tablespoons white choc bits
⅓ cup moist coconut flakes
250g cream cheese, chopped
1 cup smooth ricotta
½ cup thickened cream
½ cup icing sugar mixture
3 teaspoons finely grated lime rind
1 tablespoon lime juice
Whipped cream, to serve

1 Process biscuits, choc bits and half the coconut together until mixture is finely chopped. Transfer to a bowl.

2 Process cream cheese, ricotta, cream, icing sugar, lime rind and juice together until smooth and combined.

3 Spoon ½ cream cheese mixture between 4 x 1½ cup-capacity serving glasses. Sprinkle with ½ the biscuit mixture. Repeat layers. Dollop with whipped cream and sprinkle with remaining coconut. Serve.

NUTRITION: (per serve) 3691kJ; 66.9g fat; 45.6g sat fat; 13.8g protein; 56.7g carbs; 2.2g fibre; 140mg chol; 633mg sodium.

ICE-CREAM SUNDAE PLATTER

SERVES 4

PREP 6 minutes

COOK 14 minutes

12 small scoops vanilla ice-cream

2 large bananas, thinly sliced

50g chocolate-coated honeycomb bar, finely chopped

¼ cup slivered almonds, toasted

Caramel sauce

⅓ cup brown sugar

40g butter, chopped

⅓ cup thickened cream

Chocolate fudge sauce

100g dark chocolate, chopped

20g butter, chopped

½ cup thickened cream

1 Make Caramel sauce Place sugar, butter and cream in a small saucepan over low heat. Cook, stirring, for 4 to 5 minutes or until melted and smooth. Bring to a simmer. Simmer for 3 to 4 minutes or until slightly thickened. Pour into a small jug.

2 Make chocolate fudge sauce Place chocolate, butter and cream in a small saucepan over low heat. Cook, stirring, for 4 to 5 minutes or until chocolate is melted and sauce is smooth. Pour into a small jug.

3 Place ice-cream and banana on a platter. Drizzle with sauces. Sprinkle with honeycomb and almonds. Serve immediately.

NUTRITION: (per serve) 3142kj; fat 49.2g; sat fat 29.8g; protein 7.8g; carbs 70.7g; fibre 2.5g; chol 77mg; sodium 219 mg.

SHORTCUTS

CANNED TUNA

One 425g can of tuna, some help from us with a few cool ideas and you can create these ten fast meals.

1 TUNA MORNAY

Cook diced celery and onion in 50g melted butter. Add ¼ cup plain flour. Cook for 1 minute. Gradually add 2 cups milk, stirring constantly, until mixture boils and thickens. Stir in grated cheddar cheese and flaked tuna. Spoon mixture into an ovenproof dish. Sprinkle with breadcrumbs and drizzle with extra melted butter. Bake at 180°C/160°C fan-forced for 15 to 20 minutes or until golden.

2 SPAGHETTI WITH TUNA AND LEMON

Cook 230g dried spaghetti. Drain. Heat extra virgin olive oil in a frying pan. Add ½ small finely chopped red onion and crushed garlic and cook until softened. Remove from heat. Add hot pasta, flaked tuna, lemon rind, lemon juice and chopped flat-leaf parsley. Season with salt and pepper. Toss to combine.

3 TUNA WITH SOY AND SUSHI RICE

Cook 2 cups rinsed sushi rice following packet directions. Cool. Drizzle rice with ¼ cup sushi seasoning. Fold with a spatula to combine. Fold in 3 teaspoons soy sauce, flaked tuna, sliced green onion, toasted sesame seeds and finely chopped cucumber. Season with salt and pepper. Sprinkle with sliced toasted nori sheets, if you like.

4 POTATO AND TUNA CAKES

Boil 3 large peeled potatoes until just tender. Drain, mash and set aside to cool. Add flaked tuna, sliced green onion, chopped dill and 1½ cups grated cheddar cheese. Season with salt and pepper. Shape into patties. Coat patties in plain flour, then dip in lightly beaten egg, then coat in breadcrumbs. Refrigerate for 30 minutes. Shallow-fry until golden. Serve with salad and lemon wedges.

5 INDIAN-STYLE TUNA AND RICE

Place 2 cups basmati rice with 3 cups cold water in a saucepan over high heat. Bring to the boil, then reduce heat to low. Simmer, covered, for 10 minutes. Add chopped green beans and cook for 4 minutes or until tender. Stir in ¼ cup Indian curry paste, halved cherry tomatoes and flaked tuna. Cook until tomato softens. Stir in chopped coriander. Season with salt and pepper. Serve topped with plain yoghurt.

6 CREAMY TUNA AND BROCCOLI PASTA BAKE

Cook 3 cups pasta spirals in boiling water, adding broccoli florets towards the end of cooking. Drain. Cook chopped onion and garlic in oil. Add ¼ cup plain flour, flaked tuna, frozen peas and 2 x 375ml cans evaporated milk. Season with salt and pepper. Add pasta and combine. Spoon into an ovenproof dish and sprinkle with grated tasty cheese. Bake at 180°C/160°C fan-forced for 30 minutes or until heated through.

7 BUCKWHEAT SOBA AND TUNA SALAD

Cook buckwheat soba noodles. Refresh under cold water. Toss noodles with flaked tuna, chopped tomato, chopped avocado, juice of 1 lime and fried shallots. Season with salt and pepper.

8 NICOISE SALAD

Combine boiled chat potatoes, blanched baby green beans, flaked tuna, small black olives, halved anchovy fillets, quartered boiled eggs and torn baby cos lettuce leaves. Serve drizzled with French dressing.

9 TUNA, WHITE BEAN AND SPINACH SALAD

Combine tuna, baby spinach, halved grape tomatoes, chopped red capsicum, drained cannellini beans, chopped cucumber and chopped oregano. Season with salt and pepper. Combine olive oil, white balsamic vinegar, crushed garlic and drizzle on top.

10 TUNA BRUSCHETTA

Brush slices ciabatta bread with olive oil. Grill until golden. Combine crushed garlic, flaked tuna, finely diced tomato, chopped basil, lemon zest and baby capers. Season with pepper. Spoon onto ciabatta and drizzle with a little extra virgin olive oil.

BARBECUE CHICKEN

Pick up a barbeque chook on the way home from work. Add a few pantry essentials and whip up these delicious dinners.

1 CHICKEN WITH TERIYAKI SAUCE

Combine 1 crushed garlic clove, 2 tablespoons dark soy sauce, 2 teaspoons mirin, 2 teaspoons caster sugar and 1 tablespoon water in a saucepan. Cook until heated through. Cut hot barbecue chicken into portions. Drizzle with sauce mixture. Serve with cooked rice or soba noodles and cucumber ribbons.

2 MANGO CHICKEN COUSCOUS

Bring 1½ cups chicken stock to the boil. Add 1½ cups couscous. Stand, covered, for 5 minutes or until stock is absorbed. Fluff couscous with a fork. Add chopped barbecue chicken, toasted almonds, chopped fresh coriander, lemon zest and diced mango. Season to taste.

3 CHICKEN AND VEGETABLE RICE PAPER ROLLS

Soak rice paper rounds following packet directions. Top with shredded barbecue chicken, thinly sliced carrot, cucumber, capsicum, avocado and shredded iceberg lettuce. Roll up to enclose filling. Serve with sweet chilli sauce.

4 CHICKEN AND QUINOA WITH PESTO DRESSING

Cook 1 cup quinoa in 2 cups water, following packet directions, until liquid is absorbed. Rinse, then drain. Add shredded barbecue chicken, halved tomato medley, basil leaves, pitted kalamata olives and drained marinated fetta. Combine 2 tablespoons basil pesto with 2 tablespoons white balsamic vinegar. Drizzle over mixture. Toss to combine.

5 CHICKEN AND CHILLI SLAW

Combine shredded green cabbage, 1 shredded barbecue chicken, grated carrot, thinly sliced red capsicum, sliced green onion, torn fresh mint leaves and coriander leaves in a bowl. Combine 2 tablespoons lime juice, 2 tablespoons sweet chilli sauce and 2 teaspoons soy sauce. Drizzle dressing over salad. Toss to combine.

6 CREAMY CHICKEN AND SEMI-DRIED TOMATO PASTA

Cook sliced green onions, crushed garlic, sliced semi-dried tomatoes and wholegrain mustard in a frying pan. Add chopped barbecue chicken, cream and basil leaves. Cook until heated through. Season. Serve with cooked fettuccine.

7 CHICKEN BURGERS

Split bread rolls and toast until golden. Top with sliced barbecue chicken, sliced tasty cheese, sliced dill pickles and ready-made coleslaw. Top with roll tops.

8 CHICKEN WITH HERB SAUCE

Combine ½ cup chopped fresh herbs, including flat-leaf parsley, basil, chives plus crushed garlic, chopped capers, ½ cup extra virgin olive oil and 2 tablespoons lemon juice. Season. Cut hot barbecue chicken into portions. Drizzle with herb sauce. Serve with steamed potatoes.

9 CHICKEN, CORN AND NOODLE SOUP

Combine 1 litre chicken stock with 2 cups of water, 125g can creamed corn, 2 teaspoons soy sauce and crushed garlic in a saucepan. Bring to the boil. Add shredded barbecue chicken. Simmer until heated through. Stir in rice vermicelli noodles. Cook for 1 minute or until softened. Serve.

10 SPICY CHICKEN QUESADILLAS

Top flour tortillas with bottled salsa, baby spinach, shredded barbecue chicken and grated cheddar cheese. Top with another tortilla. Cook in a sandwich press until golden and heated through. Serve with sour cream and guacamole.

TOMATOES

Quickly pan-fried, roasted or raw, the fresh flavour of tomatoes makes them the perfect base for lots of great meals.

1 ROASTED TOMATO SOUP

Place 1kg halved roma tomatoes and 1 bulb unpeeled garlic on a baking paper-lined baking tray. Drizzle with olive oil. Roast at 180°C/160°C fan-forced for 40 minutes. Peel garlic, discard skins. Process tomato, garlic and ½ cup torn basil. Strain into jug. Cook 1 chopped onion until soft. Add ⅓ cup tomato paste, cooking for 1 minute. Stir in 2 cups chicken stock and tomato mixture. Bring to the boil. Serve.

2 CHERRY TOMATO, ANCHOVY & PINE NUT PASTA

Cook cherry tomatoes and thinly sliced garlic in olive oil until tomatoes are just starting to collapse. Toss through cooked spaghetti with finely chopped anchovy fillets, chopped flat-leaf parsley, toasted pine nuts and shaved parmesan. Season with pepper. Meanwhile, cook fresh breadcrumbs in extra virgin olive oil until golden. Sprinkle over pasta.

3 GRILLED FISH WITH SALSA

Combine 2 teaspoons ground cumin, 2 crushed garlic cloves, 1 tablespoon lime juice and 1 tablespoon olive oil in a bowl. Spoon over firm white fish fillets, turning to coat. Cook on a chargrill for 2 to 3 minutes each side or until just cooked through. Serve with a salsa of diced tomato, red onion, avocado, red capsicum, corn kernels, coriander leaves, lime juice and sweet chilli sauce.

4 TOMATO & PROSCIUTTO PIZZA

Spread pizza bases with pizza sauce. Top with thinly sliced vine-ripened tomatoes and halved grape tomatoes. Tear slices of prosciutto into pieces. Arrange on top of tomato. Sprinkle with pizza cheese. Bake at 220°C/200°C fan-forced for 15 to 20 minutes or until crisp and cheese is melted. Sprinkle with fresh basil.

5 TOMATO & GOAT'S CHEESE TARTS

Cut puff pastry sheets into 4 squares. Cut 2cm borders around the edges of squares, being careful not to cut the whole way through. Prick inside square with a fork. Spread with a little caramelised onion. Top with sliced roma tomatoes and goat's cheese. Bake at 220°C/200°C fan-forced for 15 minutes or until golden and puffed. Serve sprinkled with fresh thyme leaves.

6 WARM TOMATO & OLIVE PASTA SALAD

Cook shell pasta in boiling water until tender. Drain. Cook chopped red onion and crushed garlic in olive oil until soft. Toss through hot pasta with halved mixed olives, halved baby bocconcini cheese, quartered tomato medley, chopped oregano and balsamic vinegar.

7 ROASTED RATATOUILLE & CHICKEN TRAY BAKE

Place small chicken thigh cutlets in a large roasting pan. Arrange chopped red onion, zucchini, eggplant and red capsicum around chicken. Drizzle vegetables and chicken with olive oil. Roast at 200°C/180°C fan-forced for 30 minutes. Add whole peeled garlic cloves and cherry tomatoes to pan. Roast for 20 to 25 minutes or until chicken is golden and cooked through. Sprinkle with fresh basil.

8 RICE-STUFFED TOMATOES

Combine cooked long-grain white rice with toasted almonds, chopped raisins, ground cumin and chopped fresh coriander leaves. Season. Slice tops off vine-ripened tomatoes and scoop out flesh. Spoon rice mixture into tomatoes. Replace tops. Place in a baking dish. Spray with oil and bake at 180°C/160°C fan-forced for 20 to 25 minutes or until tender. Serve with plain yoghurt.

9 THAI FRIED RICE

Cook 1 cup jasmine rice and cool completely in the fridge. Stir-fry 1 thinly sliced onion, 400g sliced chicken breast and 2 crushed garlic cloves until cooked. Remove from wok. Stir-fry 2 lightly beaten eggs until just cooked. Add rice and chicken mixture. Add 2 tablespoons each of soy, sweet chilli and oyster sauces. Stir-fry until combined. Add 2 chopped tomatoes and 1 cup Thai basil leaves. Stir-fry until heated through.

EGGS

Economical and incredibly versatile, if you have a dozen eggs on hand you can always come up with a quick and easy family meal.

1 BAKED ANTIPASTO FRITTATA

Whisk 6 eggs, ½ cup pure cream, ⅓ cup grated parmesan and 2 crushed garlic cloves together. Layer sliced red onion, drained and chopped bottled antipasto mix, torn basil leaves and thinly sliced potato in a baking paper-lined 19cm x 29cm slice pan. Pour over egg mixture. Bake at 190°C/170°C fan-forced for 25 to 30 minutes or until set.

2 MUSHROOM & CHEDDAR OMELETTES

Pan-fry sliced mushrooms and crushed garlic. Whisk 8 eggs lightly and season with pepper. Heat a 16cm (base) non-stick frying pan over medium-high heat. Brush with melted butter. Pour in ¼ of the egg, tilting pan to allow uncooked egg to cover base. Cook for 1 minute. Top with ¼ of mushroom mixture, grated cheddar and chopped parsley. Cook until base is set. Fold in half. Transfer to a plate. Repeat with remaining mixtures.

3 QUICHE LORRAINE

Grease a 3cm-deep, 23cm (base) loose-based fluted flan tin. Line with partially thawed shortcrust pastry. Blind bake until golden. Cool. Pan-fry 3 sliced bacon rashers and 1 chopped brown onion until softened. Cool. Place in pastry case. Sprinkle with grated cheddar. Whisk 3 eggs, 1 teaspoon plain flour, 300ml pure cream and ½ cup milk together. Pour over bacon mixture. Place on a tray. Bake at 180°C/160°C fan-forced for 30 to 35 minutes or until set.

4 MEXICAN EGGS

Cook 1 finely chopped red onion and 2 crushed garlic cloves in a frying pan until softened. Add 1 teaspoon smoked paprika. Cook for 1 minute. Add 2 x 400g cans diced tomatoes, 2 tablespoons tomato paste, chopped, chargrilled capsicum and ½ cup chicken stock. Cook for 5 minutes. Make 4 holes in sauce. Crack 1 egg into each hole. Cook for 3 to 4 minutes or until eggs are set. Serve with corn chips.

5 ASIAN-STYLE FRIED EGGS

Add enough vegetable oil to a wok to come ¼ of the way up the side. Heat over medium-high heat. Crack an egg into a glass and carefully pour into the oil. Deep-fry for 1 to 2 minutes or until the egg is golden but still soft on the inside. Using a slotted spoon, carefully remove the egg from oil and drain on paper towel. Repeat with 3 more eggs. Drizzle with soy sauce, hot chilli sauce, oyster sauce and a little sesame oil. Sprinkle with bean sprouts and sliced green onion.

6 CAESAR SALAD

Brush slices of baguette with olive oil. Grill on both sides until golden. Place eggs in a saucepan. Cover with cold water. Place over medium heat. Bring to the boil, stirring often (this will centre the yolks). Reduce heat to low. Simmer for 5 minutes. Drain. Refresh in cold water. Peel and cut eggs into wedges. Arrange baby cos leaves, anchovy fillets, baguette, shaved parmesan and egg in bowls. Drizzle with Caesar salad dressing.

7 RAMEN SOUP WITH PORK

Bring chicken consommé to the boil in a large saucepan. Add ramen noodles, soy sauce, crushed garlic, sliced red chilli and grated ginger. Cook for 2 minutes or until noodles are tender. Meanwhile, place eggs in a saucepan and cover with cold water. Bring to the boil over high heat, stirring occasionally (this will centre the yolks). Reduce heat to medium. Simmer for 3 minutes. Refresh under cold water. Peel eggs and cut in half. Arrange thinly sliced snow peas and green onion in bowls. Top with noodles and thin slices of roast pork. Ladle over stock mixture and top with eggs.

8 GADO GADO

Boil eggs, remove shells and quarter. Cook ⅓ cup satay sauce, ⅓ cup coconut milk, 1 tablespoon lime juice and 1 teaspoon kecap manis in a saucepan until heated through. Steam halved chat potatoes, green beans and carrot batons. Arrange on a platter with sliced Chinese cabbage, egg and diced tofu. Drizzle with sauce.

INDEX

HarperCollins*Publishers*
First published in Australia in 2014
by HarperCollins*Publishers* Australia Pty Limited
ABN 36 009 913 517
harpercollins.com.au

HarperCollins*Publishers*
Level 13, 201 Elizabeth Street, Sydney, NSW 2000, Australia
Unit D1, 63 Apollo Drive, Rosedale, Auckland 0632, New Zealand
A 53, Sector 57, Noida, UP, India
77–85 Fulham Palace Road, London W6 8JB, United Kingdom
2 Bloor Street East, 20th floor, Toronto, Ontario M4W 1A8, Canada
10 East 53rd Street, New York NY 10022, USA

super food ideas
Australia's top-selling food magazine

Editor: Rebecca Cox
Food Editor: Kim Coverdale
Project Editor: Sally Feldman
Recipe contributors: Alison Adams; Donna Boyle; Emma Braz; Jo Anne Calabria; Kim Coverdale; Claire Brookman; Annette Forrest; Nadia French; Amira Georgy; Sharon Kennedy; Kirrily La Rosa; Cathy Lonnie; Liz Macri; Tracey Meharg; Kim Meredith; Lucy Nunes; Angela Portela; Katrina Woodman
Photography: Guy Bailey; Sam McAdam Cooper; Al Richardson; Jeremy Simons; Craig Wall; Andrew Young
Styling by Jenn Tolhurst
Cover recipe by Kim Coverdale
Food preparation by Claire Brookman

National Library of Australia Cataloguing-in-Publication data:
Dinner in a Dash/Super Foods Magazine
9780732295646 (pbk.)
Cookery–Australia.
Super Foods Magazine
Includes Index
641.552

Cover design by HarperCollins Design Studio
Cover image by Craig Wall
Internal design by HarperCollins Design Studio
Typesetting by Alicia Freile, Tango Media
Colour reproduction by Graphic Print Group, Adelaide
Printed and bound in China by RR Donnelley
5 4 3 2 1   14 15 16 17